STRAIGHT T

MW00936081

DIVORCE
REMARRIAGE

and the
innocent
spouse

counseling
for betrayed
believers

CHRISTIAN KEEL

INSPIRATIONAL BOOKS & MEDIA

DIVORCE — REMARRIAGE
AND THE INNOCENT SPOUSE:
COUNSELING FOR BETRAYED BELIEVERS
(Straight Talk Bible Study: Book One)
By Christian Keel

Streamline Inspirational Books & Media
Contact: streamline.ibm@gmail.com
www.pinterest.com/streamlinebooks/
www.twitter.com/streamline777

ISBN 13: 978-1519233691
ISBN 10: 1519233698

Published in the United States of America

First Edition 2015

To the brokenhearted

• • •

*"The righteous cry and the L*ORD *hears, and delivers them out of all their troubles. The L*ORD *is near to the brokenhearted, and saves those who are crushed in spirit."*

Psalms 34:17–18

Table of Contents

1

The Journey Ahead

"I've tried so hard to make this work. I took my wedding vows seriously. But I feel like my spouse isn't the same person I married. Honestly, I don't see how I can go much longer."

All too often, these calls come. A believer chokes out a confession like this, teetering on the brink of marital collapse. I'm asked an agonizing question:

"Do you see biblical grounds for divorce?"

"That's a good question," I reply. "But before we go on, let's invite God into our conversation."

Though I'm not a pastor or a professional therapist, many such callers have sought me out for informal biblical counsel. It's not that I have all the answers. That's why I'm so dependent upon divine guidance.

Still, those who consult me trust that no matter how hard Scripture's wisdom is to face, I'll guide them toward it as faithfully as I can. I'll pray about their heartaches with compassion. We'll talk about the need to forgive no matter what, and to explore reconciliation when possible. In an effort to increase our understanding, I'll consider the Bible's original language and context. Then, I'll be frank about how that could apply to the given situation, doing my best to avoid the pitfalls of legalism or license.

Tell you what—true respect wells in me for every believer who has the courage to set aside pride and relational pain enough to ask for godly counsel. You know why?

These are times when less devoted hearts turn from the God they've committed to follow. Many fear that He'll just make them feel guiltier than ever. They worry He'll oppose what they're bound and determined to do. Countless people run from the truth of the Gospel, reasoning that—even if they're wrong—they can beg forgiveness later.

That's why I admire those who have the courage to seek God's best for their lives, even when it seems a bitter pill to swallow. Even when that counsel leaves them sobbing. For the truly innocent spouse, those tears seem to flow either way.

If that's you, empathy fills me at the thought of what you may be suffering. This book is for you.

Spoiler Alert

I'm very pro marriage. I hate the very same things about the ravages of divorce that God does. Just like you probably do. Still, have I ever counseled that I believe a Christian has a biblically just cause to opt for divorce?

Yes. In specific circumstances.

Have there been times I've had to answer that I can't see legitimate biblical grounds? Probably just as often.

At the risk of losing readers, I'll be clear, right from the beginning. Yes, I believe there are valid biblical grounds for a Christian to divorce. But we must start by being honest with ourselves. Those looking for scriptural loopholes won't find them here. Those trying to wiggle out of vows their spouse hasn't already broken will be encouraged to stay and keep working on that marriage.

On the other hand, the Bible has much wisdom for those who are sincere about the search for clarity on this challengingly controversial subject. If you're ready to leave these often-murky waters and dive into God's crystal, healing stream—I welcome you to brave this journey with me.

Read on.

Shine the light of Scripture onto your specific situation. Invite the Holy Spirit to be your Teacher and Counselor. And in so doing, you just might be surprised at the compassionate heart the Almighty has for the plight of the innocent spouse.

As you read this book, divorce may be the farthest thing from your mind. You might be contentedly single. Perhaps you're dreaming of wedded life. Maybe you're blissfully married.

But you know someone who isn't.

It seems there are always those in our midst who are in the desperate throes of marital crisis. They may be among your family members or friends. You might see them at church or in your small group. They may come to you, desperate for just this kind of help.

This book will prepare you to offer sound counsel, straight from the pages of Scripture.

Why this study?

Every time someone seeks me out for this type of counsel, I'm reminded of what a sacred responsibility it is to offer it. The last thing I ever want to do is to play fast and loose with God's Word, or to let sympathy for any person's unhappiness lead me to take their side against the Almighty's.

I'm mindful that—informally or not—teachers (and presumably counselors) incur a stricter standard. That's something I don't take lightly. Especially when it comes to talk of putting asunder what God has joined together.

Frankly, it's with a hearty dose of trepidation that I embark upon publishing this particular Bible Study. As a devoted Christian since my youth, I believe in both the sanctity of Scripture and that mystical one-flesh union called marriage. By God's grace, my first and only marriage continues to this day.

That said, maybe you've noticed the same thing I have. Within Christian circles, we openly celebrate marriage, but the whole unsettling business of divorce is often swept under the rug. Though churches are liberally populated with those facing the devastation of divorce, few dare to openly teach on the subject.

After all, interpreting what the Bible says (and doesn't say) about divorce has fueled vigorous debate for many thousands of years. While this book espouses the most widely accepted view among Christian scholarship, there are devout theologians who differ.

It's no wonder that I can't recall ever hearing a single teaching on divorce. It's one of those wince-inducing, spiritual buzz-kill topics we tend to avoid. Naturally, we prefer feel-good messages that bolster our faith. We don't sit as well with the messier, more challenging varieties that hit too close to home. Meanwhile, divorce statistics within Christendom tick upward at an alarming rate.

So, why does a contentedly married believer like me venture into the thorny conflict over divorce? Simply put, I could not ignore it any longer.

Truth be told, years have passed since I was first asked to teach this study to a small group. At the time, a number of those who went through the study urged me to publish what I'd taught for the benefit of those outside our ranks. They requested my notes.

My response? I reasoned that those hostile to this unvarnished look at the subject wouldn't receive my counsel. Some would accuse me of legalism. Others would label me too liberal. Seemed like a lose-lose proposition to me.

So what did I do? I pulled a real Jonah. Given the hotbed of controversy, I shined the call to Nineveh on and hopped aboard a figurative ship to Tarshish. I set their requests aside. For years since, my detailed notes have remained neatly tucked in the belly of my Bible.

Until now.

Cries of the Innocent

As we begin this journey, there are some things you should keep in mind. Along the way, I'll share many snippets of anonymous, real-life accounts and statements. While related with utmost discretion, some sensitive readers may find certain elements to be disturbing. Reality is that way.

You won't find any real names in this book. This choice was made to respect and protect the privacy of those who have given me permission to share their stories. I've also deliberately altered certain non-essential details to disguise identities. Composite characterizations are used where multiple subjects have told me essentially the same story. When quotes aren't word-for-word, they still convey the distilled truth of what I've heard, often repeatedly.

Preserving anonymity in this way allows us to examine the essentials of each situation and how God's ever-relevant Word has pivotal bearing time and again. Scripture is indeed living and active. And whether its medicine seems bitter or sweet, it is life to our bones.

Biblical Gender Designations

Can you imagine how long the Bible would have been if every verse referring to one gender had been repeated just to mention the identical application to the other? Instead, Scripture often refers to a single gender, realizing readers will automatically understand when a passage applies just as readily to a man as a woman.

Granted, sometimes biblical language is gender specific. But when we come across a word translated either *man* or *men*, it's helpful to check the original language. Many biblical references often translated as *man* or *men* are actually the Hebrew word *adam,* meaning human beings of either gender. (The Greek word *anthropos* refers to men and women, too.)

In fact, in Genesis 1:6, when God said *"Let us make man [adam] in our image, according to our likeness,"* He used the word *adam* to refer to both genders. In so doing, God encompassed His plan to create a man and a woman He would unite in covenant marriage.

Writing this book has helped me understand even more why the Bible often uses gender designations in an interchangeable way. Similarly, this study is written for men and women alike, in as even-handed a manner as possible. While I'm cautious not to counsel the opposite gender in private, God has helped me to come alongside many a husband or wife, in the throes of marital crisis. I've seen male and female innocent spouses. And I don't automatically assume the guilt or innocence of either.

No matter who might be cast as the guilty spouse in any scenario I relate, in most cases, I've seen it go both ways. So, in the interest of being succinct, I won't keep repeating when gender designations can just as easily be flipped. I'll trust that you'll extrapolate my equal respect for men and women.

Four Schools of Thought

Under the umbrella of Christian scholarship, there are four main schools of thought about what the Bible permits when it comes to divorce and remarriage:

1) No Divorce / No Remarriage
2) Just-Cause Divorce / No Remarriage
3) Divorce & Remarriage—limited circumstances
4) Divorce & Remarriage—various reasons via grace

Collectively, views one, two, and four represent convictions of the minority. Views one and two are usually considered the most conservative, and view four the most liberal. The third view is held by the majority, allowing divorce and remarriage under limited circumstances, as detailed in this book.

Despite their disparities, respected Christian theologians and scholars stand in hearty agreement about the sanctity of Christian marriage, and the importance of keeping our covenant vows. With one voice, they urge believers to cleave to each other in love. They encourage us to make every effort toward forgiveness and reconciliation. However, as you can see, their interpretations differ widely about what the Bible allows (or doesn't) when marriage vows are betrayed.

As tempting as it may be to preemptively adopt any human school of thought that seems to serve our purposes, resolve with me to dig deep into Scripture's content and context first. Let's see what's really there in the Bible before cementing our views.

Remember, no matter what any earthly counselor may advise, one day you will stand before God, accountable for the choices you have made. Be brave. Search the Scriptures with me. Prayerfully study to see the full picture of divorce as the Almighty sees it, in context, from His divine perspective. Discover the path of wisdom and grace, laid out for every believer.

Pacing Ourselves for This Journey

The path to understanding God's view of divorce and remarriage will lead us all the way through the Bible. The Scriptures brim with pertinent context, building line upon line.

You may wonder what Old Testament passages mean to you today. But the better we grasp why Moses and the Prophets said what they did, the better we'll comprehend what Jesus and Paul taught later, once we get to New Testament.

Be prepared that this study is like a cross-country course. It's not a sprint. Sprinters may get to their destination sooner, but those who take the time to drink in the sights along the way will arrive much more enriched by this journey.

As tempting as it may be to race ahead for answers to burning questions about biblical grounds for divorce or when remarriage is allowed, pace yourself. We'll explore those issues fully in the latter chapters. Meanwhile, as Paul advised, study to show yourself approved. Drink in this journey every step along the way. Trust that, in the end, God's Word will provide the answers and insights you need.

The Illuminated Path of Scripture

If you're sincerely seeking to find God's view of divorce and remarriage, commit this verse to memory:

> "*For the* LORD *God is a sun and a shield; the* LORD *gives grace and glory; no good thing does He withhold from those who walk uprightly.*"
>
> *Psalm 84:11*

There's a common fear that God is a cosmic killjoy, or that adherence to Scripture will prevent your happiness, fulfillment, or freedom—especially as it pertains to your love life. Every time you're tempted to think that, remind yourself that the high road of God's Word is an illuminating sun to you.

Whether that road leads to divorce or a renewed commitment to your marriage, the Bible will shine its brilliant light on your path. God will use His living and active Word as a shield to protect you from current and future harm.

No matter whether you're the guilty or the innocent spouse, God's Word is a good thing. It's the path of grace and glory He has chosen especially for you, with your very best at heart.

•   •   •

WOULD YOU PAUSE and pray with me?

Father, thank You for being there for me—from the beginning. You gave me Your only Son to die for my sins. You've adopted me into Your family and called me Your child.

Right now, I lay all my fears, hesitations, and failures down at Your feet. Give me the courage, and the ears to hear what You're saying to me as I go through this study. Use Your Word as a lamp to my path, each step of the way.

Help me to discern Your voice clearly, Father. Rebuke the lies of the enemy. Quiet the voice of my flesh. And open my ears to the still, small voice of Your Spirit.

I trust You when You say that nothing is too difficult for You. I lean into Your wisdom and rely on Your ability to resolve everything for my best. With all that I am, I surrender to Your counsel and care.

In the name of Jesus. Amen.

2

The Innocent Spouse

"No matter what happened, I have a hard time seeing myself as the innocent spouse. It takes two, you know? Believe me, I made my share of mistakes. Things that probably contributed to the way things went. So, I wonder if there's ever any such thing as a completely innocent spouse."

Though I've lost count of the number of times that men and women have sought me out for informal biblical counsel over the years, I'd venture to say the majority fit into one of three equally excruciating categories:

1) Those longing to be married
2) Those longing to be divorced
3) Those longing to be remarried

Sad to admit, the latter two have been the most desperate. Some readily identify themselves as the innocent spouse. They explain that they're not to blame, at least not for the core problems undermining their marriages. Some are honest enough to admit ways that they've contributed to their deteriorating relationships.

After all, nobody's perfect.

No one but Jesus.

Like Paul reminds us in Romans 3:23 *"...all have sinned and fall short of the glory of God."*

Is there any such thing as a truly innocent spouse?

For purposes of this study, when we refer to the *innocent spouse*, we're not saying that any human being is free of any or all sin in the marital relationship. Unintentionally or not, we sin against our spouses in various ways. Frequently. (I hate to admit it, but I know I do this, no matter how hard I try.) So, we're not saying that any human husband or wife is without sin, as a spouse or otherwise.

By accepting that there is such a thing as an innocent spouse, we're just acknowledging that within a marriage, an imperfect human spouse may be specifically innocent of breaking the marital covenant.

Conversely, it's also possible that one or both may be considered guilty of being unfaithful to marriage vows.

If Jesus' admonition about judging makes you hesitant to assign guilt or innocence to one spouse or another, remember the Apostle Peter's exhortation of 1 Peter 4:17, that judgment should *begin with the household of God*. Through these inspired words, God enlists the help of the faithful in identifying the guilty for a just cause: the exoneration and protection of the innocent.

•   •   •

WE WON'T SPEND LONG on the broader topics of judgment, the Law, and sin in this study. So hang in there with me while we touch on them briefly, just in this chapter. These few quick reminders can help us get a clearer picture of how each of those broad-based biblical concepts give us a balanced foundation concerning divorce, remarriage, and the innocent spouse.

Thank God—because of Jesus—believers' sins are forgiven. We're freed to live under God's amazing grace. But at the same time, let's remember Jesus' own words about the Law:

"Do not think that I came to abolish the Law or the Prophets; I did not come to abolish, but to fulfill. For truly I say to you, not the smallest letter or stroke shall pass away from the Law, until all is accomplished."

Matthew 5:17–18

As we study divorce and remarriage, we'll reference the Old Testament—like Jesus did. We'll look at Mosaic Law and the Prophets as they pertain to the whole picture of what Jesus was saying when He spoke about this very controversial subject. We'll glean applicable understanding from the historical context.

We'll acknowledge the things Jesus knew that anyone in First Century Palestine would comprehend immediately, without Him having to spell it out over and over at each and every mention. Paul's Epistles will give us additional insight to fill out the whole biblical picture.

We'll assess personal cases once fully informed.

Instead of cherry-picking verses here and there, we're going to embrace a view of how the whole Bible speaks to the subjects of divorce and remarriage in concert. Together, we'll seek understanding about how all the pieces of this puzzle fit into one clear, applicable picture, for the welfare of the innocent spouse.

The Letter vs. the Spirit of the Law

You've probably heard this phrase, but have you thought about what it really means? Let's define terms:

- **The Letter of the Law:**
  Technical, legalistic adherence to the text of a regulation without factoring in context or the text's underlying meaning.

- **The Spirit of the Law:**
  The highest, most reliable standard for sin versus righteousness. It encompasses every word of the Law perfectly, in conjunction with the text's deepest and fullest meaning.

Think of the Letter of the Law on divorce as the tip of an iceberg. It's that smaller, but significant part of the whole that's easily visible on the surface. Sighting that jagged tip warns seasoned sailors that there's much more underneath to beware of when navigating treacherous waters.

As we consider the Spirit of the Law concerning divorce, we'll look at the entire iceberg—not just the tip. Not just what's underneath. Instead, we'll consider the whole picture, in context. That will help us to avoid legalism (a.k.a. the sin of the Pharisees). And hopefully, the potential impact of these decisions will ward us away from taking unbiblical license.

Take the High Road

Picture an elevated highway as you consider the whole subject of Christian divorce and remarriage. Steep drop-offs flank either side.

The biblical high road is stable and secure, its weighty foundation is sure, to its deepest layer. This road represents the entire truth of the Bible, line upon line—the Spirit of the Law. Things that are clearly stated remain in plain view as we unearth applicable context.

Just to either side of the concrete road, are those two equally perilous chasms. To one side, there's Legalism with its pharisaical, works-based adherence to the Letter, rather than the Spirit of the Law about divorce and remarriage.

To the other side, there's License, ignoring both the Letter and the Spirit of the Law. That deep ditch of License presumes upon God's forgiveness of marital sin—otherwise known as *Cheap Grace*. (For more about licentiousness, read Jude's Epistle.)

Anyone who's been there knows that navigating a misty mountain road surrounded by sheer drop-offs can be a white-knuckled ride. The wise slow down.

We're careful to avoid those hazardous edges and opt for the sure, safe center of the lane. Similarly, the fog of marital discord may mask the edges of that scriptural high road. We may find ourselves perilously close to the drop offs of legalism or license.

Let's remember, though we see through a glass darkly, God's vision is perfectly clear. He knows our hearts. He spots the boundaries between what is sin and what is not. In this light, we should carefully consider the dangers of traversing the winding mountain road of marital crisis, especially when it comes to those gray, foggy areas that run dangerously close to either chasm. And we should observe the loving warning signs that Scripture provides.

When we push the boundaries of God's directives or swerve into perceived loopholes, we can put ourselves in danger of veering into marital license, and off that safe high road God wants for us. Or when we get legalistic about divorce or remarriage, we take on the robes of the Pharisees, weighing down innocent spouses with more than God ever intended that they should suffer.

Application

In light of everything we've just said about living by the Spirit of the Law as opposed to by its Letter, let's mull over a real life conundrum. I've heard the essence of this same scenario from multiple sources:

> *"Even though my husband is the one who broke our vows, he claims it's my obligation to forgive him, and to give him another chance. Plus, he says God will hold me responsible if I'm the one who files for a divorce."*

For now, let's set the nature of the betrayal aside. Let's just use it to identify which spouse is innocent. If it's determined that the report of marital betrayal is true and the husband is the guilty party in this case, the questions raised here are threefold:

1) *Is the innocent spouse obligated to forgive?*
2) *Does forgiveness force giving another chance?*
3) *Does it matter who files for divorce?*

You may have your opinions, but take some time to consider how specific Scriptures answer each query. Resist talking about how this husband broke faith for now. Just look at those three core questions. Explore the why or why not of each.

Ask the Holy Spirit to show you the Spirit of every Law or verse that comes to mind. If you're doing this study alone, stop and think about each of these questions. If you're in a group study, open up the floor briefly for discussion before you move on.

•   •   •

READY? Okay, then.

Remembering that I'm just a flawed human being like you, here's how I'd answer these questions:

1) *Is the innocent spouse obligated to forgive?*

In light of my personal context as a forgiven sinner, plus the biblical directive to forgive one another, the answer to this question is a clear *yes*. The exhortation to freely forgive sits squarely in the middle of that high road we're called to as believers.

Initially, forgiving marital betrayal can be hard. It's even more challenging to maintain that forgiving spirit. But both are necessary prescriptions for spiritual health and emotional well-being, no matter who is guilty.

2) *Does forgiveness force giving another chance?*

This one is a bit more complex. Scripture mandates that we who have been forgiven extend forgiveness. But in cases of covenant-breaking sin, whether or not that leads to a second chance seems to be at the innocent spouse's option.

In Judaism, for instance, divorce after adultery was routine. But God set a powerful example by taking Israel back time and again, following their adulterous idolatry. Hosea also followed God's instructions to marry a prostitute, then to forgive and take her back after she betrayed him.

Even so, both Old and New Testament teachings allow room for the betrayed party to be released from marriage vows that the guilty spouse has broken. In breaching the marriage vows, the guilty spouse has effectively freed the innocent spouse from the marital covenant. This gives the innocent spouse a pivotal choice to make.

But a choice nonetheless.

As mentioned, there are those who are of the conviction that no believer can ever justly opt for a divorce. I am not one of them. As we'll discuss in chapters to come, I believe that while we have the obligation to forgive, whether or not we enter into a renewed covenant is an option—one to be weighed very carefully.

Many Christian marriages threatened by betrayal have, through God's grace, survived and gone on to thrive and bear witness of the power of forgiveness. A note of caution on this point: if we opt to forgive, we must be prepared to forgive like God does. Grace pardons the offense and moves on, letting the repentant put their sin behind them.

So, Innocent Spouse, if you do opt to give that wayward spouse of yours another chance, see that past infidelity as covered by the crimson tide of forgiveness. Grant your pardoned spouse every opportunity to demonstrate faithfulness as you venture forward. Facilitate a renewed commitment on which to rebuild.

3) *Does it matter who files for divorce?*

I'm amazed how often this question pops up. Quite literally, to suppose it matters who files burrows into the petty dirt of legalism. As it usually goes, the betraying spouse deflects his or her own guilt, attempting to tie the hands of the innocent over this technicality. It's like faulting the one who is left to sweep up after someone else has shattered a glass.

We must remember, although the circumstances that lead to divorce can be sinful and undesirable, divorce is a biblical provision for the benefit of the injured party—the innocent spouse. Who files the necessary paperwork to dissolve ties that have already been severed by another is immaterial.

There are those who may use the Letter of the Law to deflect guilt onto innocents who opt to file. But the Spirit of the Law seems clear, that the innocent spouse doesn't sin by formalizing the dissolution of vows the guilty broke.

Discussion Questions

1) *How would you define the innocent spouse?*

2) *Why is it important to identify the innocent spouse and the guilty spouse in any biblical divorce?*

3) *Should a repentant guilty spouse always be given a second chance to keep broken wedding vows?*

•   •   •

SPEAKING OF MARRIAGE VOWS, they're up next for our study. As we put together this shattered scenario, it helps to get a clear picture of exactly what's been broken.

3

The Real Deal

"Someone told me that marriage is one of the best things and one of the hardest things you'll ever do in life. Looking back, I can see how I idealized the good stuff and way underestimated how difficult the hard parts could be. Now, I thank God for the real deal of married life, both the mountaintops and the valleys. They have fashioned my character and shaped me into who I am."

When bank tellers are trained to spot fake bills, they're not given counterfeits. They're taught by exclusively handling what's real. It's been found that the more a person feels and sees what's genuine, the easier it is for that person to spot what's not.

We'll take a similar strategy in this chapter. In an effort to be responsible about the way we study divorce, we must first take a look at the realities of what divorce intends to sever: marriage. As we examine the true commitments a Christian marriage covenant entails, it'll help us to understand more readily what it means to break one.

Civil vs. Christian Marriage

The civil part of marriage that we think of today is a relatively new construct. Not that there's anything wrong with rendering to Caesar what is Caesar's, but the civil aspects serve civil functions. We give "Caesar" that marriage license fee to go on the government record as marrieds. This status qualifies us to reap certain marital benefits on things like taxes and insurance.

As important as it is to us to be lawfully wed on a civil level, for the Christian, marital vows have a deeper, overarching spiritual dimension. Whereas civil marriages may be secular, almost like a contract, Christian marriage is much more than an earthly agreement. It's a sacred covenant in which two people become one flesh in a union initiated and ordained by God. In Christian marriage, in addition to exchanging vows with each other, we also make these vows before God. We invite the Almighty into this covenant relationship.

From the very beginning, right after God created human beings, man and woman, the Bible tells us:

"For this cause a man shall leave his father and his mother, and shall cleave to his wife; and they shall become one flesh."

Genesis 2:24

Despite the fact that the serpent slithered in to mess things up for all humankind right afterward, God's intent has always been for a husband and wife to cleave to one another in enduring one-flesh union. In the deepest reality of our spirits, we become bone of one another's bones, and flesh of one another's flesh.

That Hebrew word for *cleave* is *dabaq*. It means we're supposed to cling to one another, to adhere to that person we married for life. With every ounce of strength, we hold fast. We stick together. We hang in there, no matter how that snake hisses, tempting us to let go.

It's not just *as if* we're one person once we're married. Before God, we are fully integrated into each other, like branches that have been grafted together on His vine. That fusion of our spirits takes place in an instant and deepens over time. Everything in us binds together in such a comprehensive way, more powerfully than any secular contract.

Once two branches have been grafted together and become one flesh, it's impossible to extract one from the other without severely wounding both. God never meant either part of that unified whole to go through that trauma of being severed. He meant us to remain healthy and intact as that one-flesh unit, to flourish and bear fruit.

> *"But I prayed hard before I got married. I've prayed even harder since. No disrespect, but if God means so well for me, why didn't He warn me it would come to this? Why didn't He stop the wedding?"*

We won't get bogged down with discussing free will in this study. There are other books on free will and tips on how to choose a spouse. But the bottom line as free will and choice pertain to marriage is this:

God gives us latitude.

As our loving, heavenly Father, God welcomes us to marry the spouse of our choice, only limiting us to choose from those of our Christian faith. (Even that is for our own good, so that marital unity permeates our spirits.)

On occasion, God has been known to set up a couple, like Isaac and Rebekah in Genesis 24. But notice in that instance, Rebekah was given the free will right to choose if she would marry Isaac:

"And they said, 'We shall call the girl and consult her wishes.' Then they called Rebekah and said to her, 'Will you go with this man?' And she said, 'I will go."

Genesis 24:57–58

Whether God sets a marriage up or not, His intent is for the best. Just as with Rebekah and Isaac, God's desire for our good runs even deeper than ours when we promise ourselves to a spouse.

Though life isn't always roses, God wants that happily ever after for us. He desires that one-flesh union to give us the strength we need to navigate life's inevitable storms and bear Kingdom fruit. At the same time, to call it a one-flesh union acknowledges that frail human beings are involved. We are but flesh, seeking to live up to God's holy ideal.

Meanwhile, our heavenly Father broods over us, wanting that same thing we do when we make our vows before Him: one marriage till death do us part, both spouses faithful to Him and each other, the same way He is faithful to us.

For the believer, marriage resonates with two harmonious dimensions. In addition to uniting husband and wife under God, earthly marriages are meant to reflect the profound spiritual unity of Christ with His Bride, the Church (Ephesians 5:31–32).

Sacred Vows of the Marriage Covenant

Despite the modern popularity of self-written vows, what believers pledge to each other has changed little, in essence, for many thousands of years. The charge to keep such vows echoes from the pages of the Old Testament:

> *"You shall be careful to perform what goes out from your lips, just as you have voluntarily vowed to the* LORD *your God, what you have promised."*
> *Deuteronomy 23:23*

You won't find specific marital vows like *"for better or worse, for richer or poorer, in sickness and in health"* in the Bible. Not literally. Those types of vows came into use in church weddings of the Sixteenth Century. But Deuteronomy's admonition to keep our vows stands, implicitly covering those marriage vows we choose to take. This admonition reminds us that we have taken these vows to God of our own free will, and we should be diligent to keep them.

No matter the wording of the vows taken, the Spirit of Christian marriage vows incorporate these four sacred commitments: 1) to love, 2) to cherish, 3) to honor, and 4) to keep.

Let's look at each of these core marriage vows a bit closer:

1) To love (*agapao*)

The Bible has a number of verbs that translate "*to love*" but I've highlighted this Greek one—*agapao*—from I John 3:18 for its exhortation to love not in word only, but also in deed and in truth.

To love in this way encompasses the vow to faithfully adore physically, sexually, socially, morally, mentally, and spiritually. We are to love—not just through verbal expressions—but from the heart and in consistent practice. This ardent love is the self-sacrificial umbrella under which all four basic vows operate.

2) To cherish (*sakan*)

The Hebrew word *sakan*—meaning to cherish, treasure, minister, or serve—is drawn from the intimate scenario in 1 Kings 1:2 where a young virgin was selected to nurse the aged King David. Despite their best efforts, there was no other way David could be kept warm until she lay at his side, transferring her body heat to his. The text makes it clear that there was nothing sexual about this act. Cherishing the king in this way meant to purely give of herself, to minister to him and for him.

Likewise, the vow to cherish in marriage commits to enduring, heartfelt selfless acts of care, enduring affection, and service. We are to give in this way, no matter the state or incapacity of the cherished one.

3) To honor (*timao*)

The Greek work *timao* is found in Matthew 15:4, as Jesus answered the Pharisees, digging far beneath the Letter of the Law to the Spirit of the Law. In doing so, Jesus observed one of the Ten Commandments, where we're told we must honor our parents. *Timao* means to prize, highly esteem, dignify, respect, and favor.

Think about each of those meanings as it pertains to the marital vows. Privately and publicly, husband and wife vow to humble themselves in mutual submission (Ephesians 5:21). They promise to look up to the other in each of these prescribed ways. This godly reverence is demonstrated through the words that we speak as well as the actions we take in that life-long commitment to honor each other.

4) To keep (*shamar*)

Again, the Hebrew word *shamar* harkens back to the beginning, in Genesis 2:15, when God charged Adam and Eve to keep the Garden of Eden. *Shamar* means to preserve, guard, protect, reserve, tend, and save.

The root means to hedge about, as with thorns, to guard against intruders.

At God's altar, we solemnly wed with the promise to keep ourselves solely for each other. Our words of love find demonstration as we diligently protect that sacred union from anything and anyone who would threaten it, in keeping with our vows.

• • •

THOSE FOUR COVENANTS have been around for a very long time. They have their roots in ancient Judaism.

To fulfill his wedding vows and retain the right to remain married under Mosaic Law, a husband obligated himself to provide three things for his wife. Consider how these requirements track with the four basic vows we still make today:

1) food/sustenance (to keep)
2) covering/clothing/shelter (to protect, honor)
3) cohabitation/conjugal rights (to love, cherish)

We stand before God who loves us so perfectly. We take these multi-faceted vows to love in these Christ-like ways. Each vow we take extends to every circumstance. That means every aspect of these vows applies to all of the ways we express our affection to each other. They encompass every aspect of well-being: physical, mental, practical, social, economical, emotional, and spiritual.

How long, O Lord?

For those with healthy marriages, the years may seem to fly by. But those in more challenging relationships might find themselves checking the Bible's fine print to see how long they've obligated themselves.

Unlike civil contracts that often include terms for dissolution, the term of the Christian marriage covenant endures for life. Only a spouse's death releases us from keeping this holy commitment.

> *"For the married woman is bound by law to her husband while he is living; but if her husband dies, she is released from the law concerning the husband. So then, if, while her husband is living, she is joined to another man, she shall be called an adulteress; but if her husband dies, she is free from the law, so that she is not an adulteress, though she is joined to another man."*
>
> *Romans 7:2–3*

Even as Paul clarified the lifelong term of marital commitment, you'll notice he also addressed the ramifications of when some break their vows. There may be situations where both spouses are guilty of breaking their marriage vows simultaneously. When both have broken their vows at the same time, there's no innocent spouse.

But most often, one or the other was betrayed.

If your spouse has broken marriage vows that you've faithfully kept, in God's eyes, you're the innocent spouse. That means He does not hold you responsible for your guilty spouse breaking his or her vows, or the sin involved. Instead, He looks on the innocent spouse with great compassion.

He knows the pain of betrayal first-hand.

Application

Think about how these three Mosaic requirements match God's bridal covenant with us as His Church. Whether you're doing this study alone or in a group, consider the ways God sets the example in faithfully caring for us.

Cite verses that assure us He's there for us in each of these crucial ways:

- *Provision*
- *Protection*
- *Presence in intimate relationship*

1) Think of a specific instance when God has kept these three covenants with you in a material way.

2) Consider how He's there for you spiritually in each of these ways.

•   •   •

NOW THAT WE'VE TAKEN a closer view of God's intent for Covenant Marriage—next up, we'll start looking at the ramifications for the innocent spouse when those sacred vows get broken.

4

God and the Scarlet D

"Divorce is such a stigma among Christians. It's like walking around with a big scarlet D on my chest. Every time I admit I'm divorced, I feel that stab of failure. Again and again, I face what it is to be discriminated against, to be seen as damaged goods. People's judgments are bad enough, but mostly I worry about how God sees me. I feel like I let Him down."

Any believer can tell you how difficult it is to wear that dreaded scarlet D. Though the D stands for Divorced, other D-labels dangle under that umbrella to taunt: Defective. Damaged. Dumped.

Even for the innocent spouse, the stigma seems inescapable. Face it. Time and again, they must declare their marital status, often to perfect strangers.

Reminders of the trauma are frequent—on forms to be filled out for taxes and IDs, like passports.

Some social networking sites acknowledge the awkwardness, by providing a transitional relationship status option. As if that doesn't wink to the world how rocky the road from the altar has been.

For the innocent spouse, even interacting within the body of Christ has its challenges. The topic of marital status arises regularly—one-on-one and in group settings.

Between the marrieds, families, and singles—where do separated and divorced Christians fit in? Just what does the innocent spouse say when people inquire, not knowing about those jagged scars, underlying that scarlet D?

The Battle Inside

Constantly, the innocent's mind sorts out each conversation, sifting through the horrors of what really happened versus what might be appropriate to share without gossiping.

Meanwhile, disapproval darts about as hearers fill in the blanks with speculation. Suspicion over which spouse is really to blame hangs thick in the air. Other well-meaning matchmakers push the newly broken to meet someone else, regardless of the circumstances.

When there are children involved, the innocent often find it best to stay mum about the cause of split. It hardly feels right to run down the other parent. Yet the kids are left confused about why their mom and dad parted. Unable to bring themselves to side with one parent or another, children often mistrust both.

Meanwhile, the innocent covers a host of hurts, cowering behind the shame and failure of it all. Hiding becomes a means of social and emotional survival. In pulling away from family, friends, and other believers, more scarlet Ds emerge:

Dejected. Disenfranchised. Devastated.
Desolate.

How does God see the divorced?

Social isolation exacerbates loneliness of spirit. But beyond the many challenges of human interaction, perhaps the most difficult to weather is that sense of estrangement from God many suffer. That aching fear that God is disappointed in us. Malachi's oft-misquoted words—*God hates divorce*—ring in the divorcé's ears. Questions plague, unanswered:

- *Why did God let this happen to me?*
- *Does He blame me for this divorce?*
- *Will God forgive me for my part in this?*

No doubt. Spiritually, divorce can be absolutely excruciating. It's messy no matter how amicable. On wearied knees, prayers cycle through uncertainties:

- *Is this somehow my fault?*
- *Could I have been a better spouse?*
- *Did I make an unforgivable mistake?*
- *Can my record ever be cleared?*

The unmerited ramifications of divorce on the innocent spouse are simply staggering. God knows that. And that's why He hates broken covenants so much.

A look at the Bible's original language confirms divorce's violent impact. The Hebrew word for *divorce* has the forceful connotation of cutting or hewing. It's like chopping off a limb with an ax. You know how a tree bleeds when a major branch is severed, right? But think about how brutal it can be to tear one-flesh human beings apart.

Divorce is major surgery to our spirits, akin to amputation. No matter how skillful the surgeon, it's impossible to separate what God has joined without severe trauma. There's a lengthy healing process. Phantom pain from that lost limb haunts. Scars remain. No matter how innocent the spouse.

Even more than an adoring earthly parent would, God looks upon His innocent, injured children with abounding compassion. His heavenly heart grieves for those who have been betrayed. Our Father longs to gather the broken up, into His arms of love. How can we know this? Because the Bible tells us that He's been there.

Is divorce always a sin?

Again, we'll look to the Bible for answers. In its pages we find two innocent spouses whose thoughts turned to divorce—one when infidelity was misperceived, and the other when unfaithfulness was confirmed.

It's easy to read right over Matthew 1:19, where Joseph considered secretly breaking his engagement to Mary when he mistakenly thought she'd become pregnant with another man's child. (In Joseph's day, a divorce was required to end a betrothal or marriage.) The story goes on to tell how God sent an angel to assure Joseph that Mary had conceived as a virgin, by the Holy Spirit. But before that—while Joseph quietly made plans to divorce Mary—Matthew characterized Joseph as a righteous man, an innocent spouse contemplating divorce.

The Scriptures provide an even clearer answer to why divorce cannot always be a sin. The reason? Because our sinless God divorced Israel on grounds of her adultery. Take a moment to digest that.

Because of His Bride's unfaithfulness, God became a righteous divorcé. Here's where the Almighty declared it, through a major Prophet:

> *"And I saw that for all the adulteries of faithless Israel, I had sent her away and given her a writ of divorce, yet her treacherous sister Judah did not fear; but she went and was a harlot also."*
>
> *Jeremiah 3:8*

Some are quick to point out that only a few verses later, God told Israel that He'd take her back, if only she'd acknowledge her sin against Him and repent. Like the picture of betrayal and forgiveness that became Hosea's life, God ultimately had mercy on His wayward Bride. But that doesn't change the fact that justice was righteously meted out first, before God graced Israel with another chance.

Isaiah's prophecy confirms this spiritual divorce, once again mentioning that God justly initiated the proceeding:

> *"Thus says the LORD, 'Where is the certificate of divorce, by which I sent your mother away? Or to whom of My creditors did I sell you? Behold, you were sold for your iniquities, and for your transgressions your mother was sent away.'"*
>
> *Isaiah 50:1*

Putting Away of Idolatrous Wives

This wasn't the only time God became party to ending an adulterous marriage. As the Old Testament recorded, the prophet Ezra was completely appalled to hear the following report:

> "...the princes approached me, saying, 'The people of Israel and the priests and the Levites have not separated themselves from the peoples of the lands, according to their abominations... 2 For they have taken some of their daughters as wives for themselves and for their sons, so that the holy race has been intermingled with the peoples of the lands; indeed, the hands of the princes and the rulers have been foremost in this unfaithfulness.' "
>
> *Ezra 9:1–2*

Indeed, Ezra was so distraught upon hearing this news that he tore his robe. He literally pulled his own hair from his head and beard. In utter shame, he fell on his knees before God.

Ezra cried out to God for the rest of the day, till the evening. Desperately he repented, in humiliation over the idolatrous intermarriages that had taken place under his watch. As a nation, they'd willfully indulged in the idolatrous practices of their pagan wives, abominations against God. Especially mortifying was the fact that their leaders were among the worst offenders in this widespread unfaithfulness.

Chapter Ten records how a large assembly of men, women, and children gathered around Ezra as he prostrated himself before God over their guilt. He wept bitterly that they'd broken their sacred covenant by marrying outside their faith and giving into their atrocious idolatries. It was mass spiritual adultery, in violation of the Seventh Commandment.

Ezra knew the gravity of this sin and the peril in which it put the entire nation. That's why he was so beside himself, pleading for wisdom from God about how to deal with the situation. While Ezra was earnestly praying, asking God what should be done, a man named Shecaniah came to him with this answer:

> *"We have been unfaithful to our God, and have married foreign women from the peoples of the land; yet now there is hope for Israel in spite of this. 3 So now let us make a covenant with our God to put away all the wives and their children <u>according to the counsel of my lord</u> [the* LORD *God] and of those who tremble at the commandment of our God, and let it be done according to the law. 4 Arise, for this is your responsibility, but we will be with you; be courageous and act."*

Ezra 10:2–4

Ezra immediately recognized Shecaniah's counsel as God's answer to his desperate prayer. As you can see, Shecaniah urged Ezra to covenant with God to put all their foreign wives and their children away. As these pagan marriages weren't documented by proper Jewish marriage certificates, there was no need for bills of divorcement. They were simply to sever ties by "putting away" their foreign wives.

Notice that though the NASB version translates Shecaniah's underlined words as "*according to the counsel of my lord,*" in the original Hebrew, Shecaniah used the word *Adonay*, which was only used as a proper name for the LORD God. That's how we know that Shecaniah delivered this counsel as coming from God Himself. This included his charge that it was Ezra's responsibility as God's prophet to stand up, be courageous, and act upon it.

And act, Ezra did.

Scripture tells us that Ezra started at the top, with those leaders who had been the greatest offenders. He went directly to the priests and the Levites. Ezra compelled them to take an oath to abide by every word of Shecaniah's counsel from the LORD.

Next Ezra called all the exiles to assemble in Jerusalem. Anyone who refused to come would have to forfeit all his possessions and be thereafter excluded from their number. The threat of that penalty was severe enough to bring all the people into the open square, in front of the house of God. They stood there in heavy rain, trembling at the weight of this matter. Then Ezra stood before all of them and said:

> *"You have been unfaithful and have married foreign wives adding to the guilt of Israel. Now, therefore, make confession to the LORD God of your fathers, and do His will; and separate yourselves from the peoples of the land and from the foreign wives."*
>
> *Ezra 10:10–11*

There are those who underplay the implications of this passage, arguing that this mass marriage-ending command was merely Shecaniah's idea, not prompted by the Almighty. But clearly, as God's prophet, Ezra didn't see it that way. He received Shecaniah's message as inspired by and from the LORD, and he decisively acted upon it. God positioned this instruction as an imperative to *"do His [God's] will"* by separating themselves from their idolatrous wives.

This divinely ordered mass "putting away" of wives and children may seem harsh to some, but it was the only way to cleanse the nation of their adultery against their previous covenant with God. It also compelled the men to return to the innocent Hebrew wives they'd married and abandoned.

Who was the Innocent Spouse?

Those who check the long list of adulterers cited in Ezra 10:17–44 may wonder—with so many guilty husbands and wives—who was the innocent spouse? Again, against His will, the Almighty stood in that role.

Even faced with Israel's repeated harlotries, God heard Ezra's tearful cries. Through the Holy Spirit, He sent an inspired answer through Shecaniah, giving Ezra a way out of their marital mess. God would take His wayward Bride back, if she would confess her sin, turn away from her affairs, and return to fidelity with Him.

Forgiving Infidelity

In our humanity, it can be hard to imagine how such a rampantly cheating spouse could be forgiven, how trust could ever be extended after such blatant unfaithfulness. But then again, God is no ordinary spouse. He's the unfailingly merciful Lover of our souls.

When the Bible says God understands our weaknesses—that He has endured every trial that we have, yet without sin—that includes the betrayal leading to divorce (Hebrews 4:15). He even knows what it's like when adulteries produce extramarital children.

Better than any of us, God knows the heartache of infidelity first-hand. He understands what it's like to be betrayed, because God was the Innocent Spouse in the divorce from Israel. He was also the Innocent Spouse in the debacle with Ezra.

The Almighty's Grounds

In both cases, the grounds were the same breach of their covenant relationship. Adultery—in the form of idolatry—justified both the divorce in Jeremiah 3:8 and the command through Ezra to put away their pagan wives.

When God called Israel's unfaithfulness to their covenant relationship treachery, He identified their idol worship as a spiritual form of adultery (Jeremiah 3:20). This compounded Israel's physical adulteries.

Yes, despite Israel's frequent harlotries, God remained faithfully true to her. But His just divorce with its formalizing certificate remains forever on the record in the Bible. It rings with heartfelt empathy and encouragement for every innocent spouse.

To this day, the scarlet D God still wears for us drips with the blood of His Son. But on His ever-gracious chest, that scarlet D takes on new meaning:

Determined.

Dedicated.

Devoted.

Divorce is not a sin for the innocent spouse. Not when it's justified by the broken vows of the guilty. Clearly, though divorce isn't always a sin, it always results from sin on the part of the unfaithful spouse.

Yes, God hates it when covenant marriages end in divorce. Divorce was never what God intended for those He united for life. But God has dual covenants to consider:

1) *Vows spouses make to each other*
2) *Vows God has made to us*

Sometimes God's covenant of faithfulness to the innocent supercedes. That prompts God to allow for things He never wanted. In Moses' day, rampant hardheartedness prompted the Almighty's hand. We'll study Mosaic Law on divorce in context later. But for now, suffice it to say that divorce became necessary as a means of God keeping His husbandly covenant to the innocent spouse.

Think about it.

Seriously.

What kind of heavenly Husband would God be if He didn't ardently rise to the defense of His innocent Bride?

"For your husband is your Maker, whose name is the LORD *of hosts; and your Redeemer is the Holy One of Israel, who is called the God of all the earth.* **6** *For the* LORD *has called you, like a woman forsaken and grieved in spirit, even like a wife of one's youth when she is rejected, says your God.* **7** *For a brief moment I forsook you, but with great compassion I will gather you.* **8** *In an outburst of anger I hid My face from you for a moment; but with everlasting lovingkindness I will have compassion on you, says the* LORD *your Redeemer."*

Isaiah 54:5–8

Sometimes, it feels like forever before the sin that leads to divorce captures God's attention and ignites His righteous anger. Relief can seem distant. In those moments, it appears He's forgotten us, but these verses reassure us to hang on and know this truth for a certainty:

He is there for us.

Always.

Through Isaiah, God reminds us that redemption may tarry, but it is on its way. And those interludes we endure are relatively brief in comparison to the everlasting compassion He shows to the grieved and forsaken spouse.

Why would God allow what He hates?

Permission to divorce was never meant to condone the unjustified practice of divorce. Instead, it was God's way of providing for the innocent who have been betrayed by the sin of the hardhearted.

When answering this question, remember that there's a big difference between God's forbearance in permitting divorce and His unqualified approval of the fact that divorce proved necessary in a fallen world. Divorce in and of itself isn't always a sin, not for the innocent. But there is always sin involved against one spouse or the other. Sometimes both.

God's anger is righteously directed at the unjust breaking of the marital covenant. He despises the unfaithfulness that shatters the one-flesh vow. He loathes seeing anything hurt the innocent, the way unfaithfulness and divorce do.

God never wanted divorce. It was never His intent that the innocent suffer that wrenching pain of betrayal. But in this broken world, filled with flawed husbands and wives, those sins that bring about divorce happen. Because of the many hardhearted acts of the guilty, God permitted a way out for the sake of the innocent spouse.

Maybe that's hard to imagine, but it's not the first time God has provided recourse for victims of sinners. Ever the champion of the disenfranchised, betrayed, and oppressed—our Father is a God of justice, rising to the defense of the innocent.

Real-life Case Study

Still having trouble wrapping your head around how God could possibly permit some believers to divorce? Consider this description of a true scenario that I encountered, tragically in Christian circles:

> *"I can't tell you how appalled I was when I realized my spouse was sexually abusing our child. Right in our own home. As hard as it was to face up to what had to be done and why, I reported this horrendous crime. For the sake of my innocent child, I had to. I'd been faithful to my spouse. I never wanted a divorce. But divorce helped me to protect my child from further abuse. It set us free to start a new life."*

Now, consider this same circumstance from God's point-of-view. Think of how our Father in heaven feels when He witnesses these unthinkable sins against His beloved children. Surely, righteous anger must burn.

Yes, God hates it when these things happen.

He never wanted it to be that way.

But in this present darkness, where covenant-breaking abominations like this take place, God lovingly permits divorce. This is purely as a means of rescue for the innocent.

Is unjust divorce unforgivable?

Not according to the Bible. Still, the sins that can lead to it are not ever to be taken lightly. Hebrews delivers a sobering warning to those who would violate their vows. Judgment awaits:

> "*Let marriage be held in honor among all, and let the marriage bed be undefiled; for fornicators and adulterers God will judge.*"
>
> *Hebrews 13:4*

There's no way around it.

Biblically, breaking the one-flesh covenant is sin. Serious consequences and continuing impact await. This is a hard truth the guilty spouse may try to dodge, but cannot ignore in the end. Yet the overwhelming message of the Gospel is that even these sins can be forgiven at the foot of the cross.

The Samaritan woman Jesus met at the well in John 4:5–29 was a serial divorcée and adulterer, yet His love and mercy extended to her. Jesus offered her that cleansing Living Water and revealed Himself as the Messiah.

In John 8:1–11, again we see Jesus' compassion on the guilty—this time on the woman caught in the very act of adultery. Though the scribes and Pharisees brought her to Jesus for judgment, Jesus didn't condemn her. Instead he set the example for the religious elite, essentially reminding them that all have sinned and fallen short of God's glory. Then—ever so graciously—he turned to the woman, assuring her that He didn't condemn her. Instead, he encouraged her to go on with life forgiven. He advised her to sin no more.

Frequently Asked Questions

Q: *Does divorce fall short of God's glory and intent?*
A: Yes. God wants one-flesh marriages to thrive.

Q: *Is divorce always a sin?*
A: No. An innocent spouse may be party to a divorce caused by a guilty spouse.

Q: *Why did God divorce Israel?*
A: Because they broke faith with Him by their evil acts, adulteries, and idolatry.

Q: *Why was God released from His marital covenant?*
A: He was the innocent spouse.

Q: *Did God sin in divorcing Israel?*
A: No. God remains sinless despite this just divorce.

Q: *Is it sin for an innocent spouse to initiate divorce proceedings against a guilty spouse?*
A: Not in and of itself, but great care should be taken not to sin in how the process is navigated.

Q: *Can those guilty of marital unfaithfulness be forgiven?*
A: Thank God, yes. Our covenant-keeping Father leads the way in extending abounding forgiveness. Sincerely repentant sinners can find grace and help from our ever-merciful Savior (1 John 1:9).

•   •   •

READY TO JOURNEY back in time? In the next chapter, we'll study the Bible's first dealings with divorce in the books of Moses.

5

Moses and Divorce

"I was devastated to discover my wife had betrayed me again. Going through that divorce was the darkest, most desolate time of my life—like being in a cave. Had it not been for godly friends coming alongside me, I don't know how I would have survived it."

Oh, the heartache of infidelity.

Better than anyone, God knows what that's like for the innocent spouse. He knows the searing pain of betrayal, the challenge of forgiveness, the loneliness of spirit. He sees the need for godly consolation and aid.

Things sure have changed since God initiated marriage between Adam and Eve in the Garden. The Fall caused the First Couple's expulsion from Eden.

And their sin compromised God's intents and ideals. This trickled down to marriage, the closest of human covenant relationships.

How did divorce come about?

Some might wonder what a basic knowledge of the history of Jewish divorce law might have to do with contemporary Christians. But even those of us who live under the New Covenant of Grace can benefit from a brief look at what led up to where we are today.

Jesus referenced Moses' divorce directives. And some Old Testament context will give us a framework to better understand what Jesus said in the Gospels.

In the Bible, the first reference to divorce appears in Moses' day, after he led the children of Israel out of Egypt. Divorce was unheard of in Israel prior to that time. It stands to reason that at some point during their 400 years of slavery, Israel may have adopted the Egyptian practice of divorce. They developed their own writ of divorcement to accommodate breaks of the marital covenant within their ranks.

Moses' generation may have been born into a pre-existing culture where divorces were already common. It's quite likely that Israel's practice of formalizing a Hebrew divorce with a writ pre-dated Moses' first mention in Deuteronomy.

Why did Moses let divorce continue?

The fact that Moses had to address this subject hints that Israel's repeated adulteries weren't only of the idolatrous variety. Sadly, marital unfaithfulness proliferated among the freed nation.

Men had all the rights in those days. Unloved wives suffered neglect, abuse, even loss of life at the hands of husbands who just wanted out, often to pursue others. So Moses, under God's authority, intervened on behalf of the innocent spouse.

It's clear that neither God nor Moses condoned divorce. Rather, it was permitted to prevent the greater evils that could befall a neglected Hebrew wife. In that day, a woman couldn't get a job. She needed a faithful husband's provision to survive. The short bill of divorce Moses affirmed gave spurned wives legal proof of their eligibility to remarry.

Divorce Decrees in Jewish Law

Though it's not certain precisely when the writing of divorce certificates began in Israel, the practice is referenced in the Talmud (the collective basis for Jewish Law, expounding on subjects outside the Hebrew Scriptures).

In Judaism, divorce has been accepted as an undesired reality of life for thousands of years. Under Judaic laws, a husband could divorce his wife with or without reason. Their writings specify that a man could divorce a woman because she ruined a meal, or even because he had come to find another woman more beautiful.

Given the ramifications of adultery on the part of a husband or wife, the *No Fault* concept of divorce has long been recognized within Judaism. To prevent men from divorcing their wives without due financial consideration, rabbinical authorities oversaw proper documentation. Divorce kept neglected, innocent wives from starving by freeing them to remarry.

Only husbands were allowed to initiate a divorce in Moses' day. Hebrew wives could neither initiate nor prevent the process.

They were literally at the mercy of the men.

Even if a man were presumed dead in battle—without proof of death, his wife remained bound to him. For this reason, it became customary for a man on his way to war to give his wife a provisional certificate of divorce, in the event he perished on the battlefield under circumstances that couldn't be proven.

What did a divorce decree say?

In the Talmud, a writ of divorce was called a "scroll of cutting off" (*sefer k'ritut*). Today, this ancient writ is known as a *"Get."* Compared to today's far wordier decrees, the Jewish *Get* was a short fill-in-the-blanker. In modern English, it would have read like this:

On the _____ day of the week _____ in the month _____ in the year _____ from the beginning of the world, according to the common computation in the province of _____, I _____ the son of _____ by whatever name I may be known, of the town of _____ with entire consent of mind, and without any constraint, have divorced, dismissed, and expelled _____ daughter of _____ by whatever name you are called, of the town which has been my wife's to this day. But now I have dismissed you _____ the daughter of _____ by whatever you are called, of the town of _____, so as to be free at your own disposal, to marry whomsoever you please, without hindrance from anyone, from this day for ever. You are therefore free for anyone (who would marry you). Let this be your bill of divorce from me, a writing of separation and expulsion, according to the Law of Moses and Israel.

_____, the son of _____, witness

Early Hebrew legislation references the use of the Jewish *Get*, formalizing a divorce and providing for remarriage, all in less than a page. Under Jewish law, man and wife are still considered married till the *Get* has been received by the woman.

Though you won't find the text of a Jewish G*et* in the Bible, use of this legal certificate of divorce was acknowledged by Moses. It was also referenced by God through the Prophets—Isaiah and Jeremiah.

Three Strikes, You're Out

If you think that Jewish *Get* looks short, it at least took a lot longer than the verbal divorces declared in that day, terminating marriages in a matter of seconds. Many ancients followed the law of Hammurabi. This allowed that a husband could divorce his wife by simply repudiating her three times in succession:

"*I repudiate you*" (or "*I divorce you*") three times, and the deed was done.

When those words popped out, even in the heat of the moment, the woman could be forced out of the home without any proof of divorce. This left her on the street, open to suspicion of and penalties for adultery if she should remarry.

That's why Moses' Law required the husband to give his wife a bill of divorcement. This was for the expressed purpose to allow for her legal remarriage. Whether the husband or wife were the innocent spouse, this protected the victim's rights.

Formalizing the divorce also took longer than the sometimes rashly spoken triple repudiation. This allowed cooling off time and the possibility of reconciliation while legal matters were being finalized through the religious authorities.

•　　•　　•

THOUGH IT WAS NOT GOD'S INTENT that we would break marital vows, because of our fallen nature and hardness of heart, Moses was inspired to give Israel regulatory instructions. Moses didn't promote divorce any more than God did. Moses simply permitted divorce as a way of helping the innocent spouse.

The fact that Jesus said Moses "suffered" to permit divorce indicated Moses' reluctance about what he knew he must do. He had a rampant problem to curb. Moses was compelled to prevent a severe injustice, lest it continue to befall the innocent.

Judgments Moses handed down assured justice, no matter whether the husband or wife proved innocent. Notice how this directive from Moses protected the innocent while also serving as a cautionary deterrent for both husband and wife:

> *"If any man takes a wife and goes in to her and then turns against her,* **14** *and charges her with shameful deeds and publicly defames her, and says, 'I took this woman, but when I came near her, I did not find her a virgin.'* **15** *Then the girl's father and her mother shall take and bring out the evidence of the girls' virginity to the elders of the city at the gate."*
>
> *Deuteronomy 22:13–15*

Since the penalty for a wife's adultery was stoning, such charges were gravely serious (v. 21). Verses like these reveal the context. Moses spoke to real life situations that were actually occurring in Israel as he led that growing nation. Though *The Ten Commandments* prohibited the bearing of false witness, clearly that sin was still committed in their midst— enough for Moses to curb this potentially deadly form of it.

Even if a woman weren't condemned to stoning as punishment, being divorced for unfaithfulness could prove a virtual death sentence. After all, guilty or innocent, the divorced so-called "adulteress" had few prospects.

With no right to work or own property in that day, most women had only two options: starve or sell their bodies into prostitution to feed themselves and any children who had also been put out on the street.

The dual wisdom of Moses' command was keen. At the same time as this protected innocent wives from false charges, the prospect of stoning also dissuaded young Hebrew women from promiscuity. It shielded those who remained pure from being unjustly divorced.

What if it turned out that the husband accused his wife falsely? Here's what Moses said:

> "...the elders of that city shall take the man and chastise him, and they shall fine him a hundred shekels of silver and give it to the girl's father, because he [the husband] publicly defamed a virgin of Israel. And she shall remain his wife; he cannot divorce her all his days."
>
> Deuteronomy 22:19

Some may wonder why an adulterous wife's punishment (stoning) seems much harsher than the husband's penalty for bearing false witness (public chastisement, a fine, and being banned for life from divorcing his wife). But look at it this way: if the husband were stoned for his false accusations, that would leave his innocent widow's life in peril. Having lost her virginity, she'd be perceived as unclean, spoiled, not so marriageable.

Therein lies the wisdom in Moses' judgment. Public chastisement of the man defamed him. It made up for publicly defaming his chaste wife and cleared her name. The fine offset the humiliation and expense the wife's parents would have borne in proving their daughter's innocence. Being banned from ever divorcing the exonerated wife bound the guilty husband to make it up to his wife by taking care of her for the rest of her life. It kept her off the streets.

Stoning wouldn't serve the wife, not as well as Moses' "life without possibility of divorce" sentence did. To the contrary, if the husband's charges proved true in that culture, he was freed to remarry, either by the stoning death of his wife or by divorcing her.

• • •

JUST TWO CHAPTERS LATER, Moses was inspired to elaborate further about divorce law. In their growing nation, this problem simply wouldn't go away.

Let's take a look at Moses' text. Imagine the marital strife that must have led to this complex declaration of Scripture:

> "*When a man takes a wife and marries her, and it happens that <u>she finds no favor in his eyes because he has found some indecency in her</u>, and he writes her a certificate of divorce and puts it in her hand and sends her out from his house,* **2** *and she*

leaves his house and goes and becomes another man's wife, **3** *and if the latter husband turns against her and writes her a certificate of divorce and puts it in her hand and sends her out of his house, or if the latter husband dies who took her to be his wife,* **4** *then her former husband who sent her away is not allowed to take her again to be his wife, since she has been defiled; for that is an abomination before the* LORD, *and shall not bring sin on the land which the* LORD *your God gives you as an inheritance.*"

Deuteronomy 24:1–4

Quite a mouthful, huh? We'll sort through multiple issues Moses touched on in this passage.

First, a little context. Within ancient Israel, men thanked God regularly that they weren't born as either a woman or a dog. Women were like property. Some were actually slaves whose status became elevated to *wife* after espousal.

Rather than permitting *No Fault* divorce, verse one cites the biblically justified cause for which Moses permitted a man to divorce his wife. Moses was inspired to allow that a man may write his wife a bill of divorcement if she "*finds no favor in his eyes because he has found some indecency in her.*"

Finding some unseemly thing didn't obligate the man to divorce his wife, but if her indecent flaw were so profound that he could no longer look upon her with favor sufficient to keep his marital vows to her, he could write her a bill of divorcement. There are multiple ways hardness of heart could have come into play:

1) *a husband or wife's betrayal*
2) *a husband's unwillingness to forgive*
3) *a wife's unloving behavior*
4) *a husband divorcing for a trivial reason*

Take a look at that word for the key justification for divorce: *indecency*. The Hebrew word (*ervah*) translated *indecency* in the NASB literally means *nudity*.

Obviously, Moses was not saying that a man could divorce his wife if he discovered her naked. That tells us we should look deeper, into the figurative meaning of this word, in context.

Figuratively, the Hebrew word *ervah* has each of these meanings:

1) *Disgraceful, shameful, or improper behavior*
2) *Dishonorable defect, flaw, or blemish*
3) *Exposed uncleanness (often sexual impurity)*

Again, this is not to say that Moses meant for a man to divorce his wife for any trifling form of indecency. For example, if a wife got a skin blemish, that wouldn't rightfully be considered an indecent flaw or a dishonorable defect. If she soiled her clothes working in their field, that didn't make her unclean. Not in the eyes of God.

Granted, many men took advantage of petty ways to say their wives lost favor with them. They divorced on technicalities, justifying their actions by citing the Letter of the Law.

However, those who observed the Spirit of the Law of Moses knew that the indecency justifying divorce had to be of a much more substantial, vile, or perverse nature in order to be considered applicable under Mosaic Law.

What constitutes a dishonorable defect today?

Various sexual sins against a spouse are readily understood as applicable "indecencies" under *ervah*. However, some may wonder what would quality as a dishonorable defect, disgraceful flaw, or improper behavior in the modern era.

Let's be clear. No illness, disfigurement, or disability that's outside a spouse's control would qualify. To legitimately fall under the meaning of *ervah*, a flaw must have a disgraceful or dishonorable component. These flaws go beyond the physiological or accidental to hardhearted intention and behavior. These are significant, shameful defects in a person's character. They result in serious sins that put the welfare of the household in jeopardy, and thereby violate the marriage covenant.

Sometimes, they can prove dangerous.

For example, suppose a wife suffered from postpartum depression after the birth of her child. In and of itself, that should never be considered a sin or a dishonorable defect in a woman's character. It's a sickness the innocent husband should lovingly nurse his wife through. However, suppose that a chronically depressed mother refused all reasonable treatment and therapy. What if she became so disturbed that she tried to kill her husband or child? When a spouse rebuffs treatment for a mental illness or disorder, resulting in depraved plots or criminal acts—that adds up to a dishonorable flaw in character.

Maybe a husband has some sort of substance addiction. Of course, it's an honorable thing for an addict to seek treatment. But if a spouse rejects rehabilitation—if he indulges his dependence to the point where he becomes neglectful, physically abusive, or a criminal—that's dishonorable. It's shameful to choose anything that violates the marital covenant to provide for and protect the innocent spouse. And if his disgraceful actions land him in prison, he's broken his vow to cohabitate.

In Moses' day, fornication and adultery were probably the most common forms of dishonorable behavior against a spouse. But it also seems that, as below, other truly shameful character flaws could have applied.

Modern Case Study

Consider how this contemporary true scenario could have applied under Moses' ruling:

> *"My husband indulged himself in a very rare, sexually-charged fetish. It's known as paraphilic infantilism. Quickly, his obsession with dressing, behaving, and needlessly using diapers like a baby took over our lives and undermined our marriage. He would have liked me to participate with or at least accept his devotion to infantilism, but I just couldn't. So, he found other men over the Internet to entertain this sensuality. It became impossible for us to have normal marital relations. And he was completely unwilling to get help or change."*

Can you imagine how abandoned this wife must have felt in her marriage? As extreme as this true account may seem to some, it's included here to illustrate how, in addition to conventional forms of sexual immorality or adultery, there are other serious issues that some may have considered sexually improper or unfaithful behavior under Moses' law.

•   •   •

MOSES MAY NOT HAVE BEEN dealing with this exact type of modern scenario in his day, but tour the Old Testament. We see that people then were every bit as unfaithful to one another as they can be today.

Wherever guilt rested, Moses knew something had to be done for the welfare and protection of every innocent spouse. That's why Moses allowed that a man with just cause could put a divorce certificate into his wife's hand and send her out of his house.

At that time, the man would be obliged to return whatever dowry had been specified in their marriage certificate. This ancient predecessor of today's pre-nuptial agreement guaranteed that the rejected woman would not be put out on the street empty handed.

Remarriage after Interim Marriage

Later in Deuteronomy 24:1–4, Moses' prohibition against remarrying a wife once she'd been "*joined to another*" appears. This guarded against the man going back into sexual relations with a woman who had been married to another man since.

The ban also prevented a common form of financial treachery. It removed the incentive of the husband to remarry for any dowry or inheritance his former wife may have acquired in the course of her intervening marriage and divorce, or widowhood.

Clearly, this passage deals with possible sins of both husbands and wives. Though it's overt about the possibility of sinful wives, context unearths the way this passage addresses a common form of treachery among Israel's husbands.

Especially as men traveled away from home, many began to take up with other women amongst their pagan neighbors. They neglected their Hebrew wives. To prevent the greater evil of harm coming to those innocent, abandoned women, Moses enforced specific requirements for marriage. He provided divorce as a way out for the innocent. These requirements stand as part of the inspired counsel of Scripture, delivered by an esteemed prophet of God.

Three Requirements for Marriage

To review, remember there were three requirements on Moses' list for each husband. A man had to give his wife all three things in order to keep his marriage vows and to retain the right to remain married to a woman. At minimum, the Jewish marriage certificate (*Ketubah*) required the man to provide:

1) food (provision, support)
2) clothing (shelter/protection)
3) cohabitation (with conjugal rights)

Originally, these requirements were specified for men who married slaves. But Moses' same directives were regularly applied to non-slave marriages as well, thus fulfilling the Spirit of the Law. (Many laws multitasked like this to cover a variety of applicable situations, rather than repeatedly writing the same thing out to apply to every scenario.)

Locate and highlight each of Moses' three basic requirements in this passage (*her* refers to the original Hebrew wife):

> "*If he takes to himself another woman, he may not reduce her food, her clothing, or her conjugal rights. And if he will not do these three things for her, then she shall go out for nothing, without payment of money.*"
>
> *Exodus 21:10–11*

Close inspection of Moses' time reveals the kind of hardheartedness that led Moses to take up the cause of abandoned women who had no right or means to provide for themselves. Remember how Jesus told the Pharisees that Moses gave them divorce because of their hardness of heart? (Matthew 19:8.)

Hardness of heart toward these innocent wives manifested with great treachery. Dreadfully, some husbands went so far as to secretly murder their Hebrew wives to evade fulfilling those three marital obligations. Other men held their wives hostage to buy their way out of the marriage. That's why Moses specified that these impoverished and innocent wives were to be freed from their husbands without payment.

Even when liberated, the betrayed original spouse and any children were left in a perilous predicament. Remember, women didn't have the rights they do today. They were entirely dependent upon their husbands for sustenance. Unless her husband gave her a certificate of divorce, freeing her to marry another man, she was virtually doomed.

That's why those three minimum requirements of provision, protection, and conjugal cohabitation were specified on each Jewish marriage certificate. And in the interest of the wife's welfare, the divorce certificate specifically allowed for remarriage under the same conditions. Most women would've had no other means of righteous support if they weren't allowed to remarry.

Just as Jesus reminded the Pharisees, indeed, it was hardness of heart that prompted Moses to state minimum provision requirements for marriage and to provide for divorce and remarriage under certain circumstances. Jesus stepped in as champion and defender, to protect the innocent spouse.

As Christians, we live under the New Covenant, but sadly some of the same treacheries against marriage still take place. God's righteous anger is still raised at the guilty in defense of the innocent spouse.

Discussion Questions

1) How would you define an indecent blemish or dishonorable behavior under Moses' law?

2) Are any of Moses' laws regarding marriage and divorce still relevant to Christians today?

•   •   •

HAVE YOU HEARD PEOPLE misquote and misapply Malachi's original language by saying that God hates divorce? We'll focus on that lightning rod passage in the next chapter.

6

Priests Rebuked

"A victim of domestic violence came to me, terrified because her priest told her she shouldn't leave her abusive husband. In addition to beating her, this man also illegally produced a controlled substance in their home. I took her to meet with my pastor, confident that he would give this believer wiser guidance. Shockingly, my pastor also counseled this battered woman to stay with her husband. He reasoned that even if she died at her husband's hands, she'd be with Jesus and God would be glorified. Horrified, I counseled her to ignore her priest and my pastor and go to a safe house."

Sadly, such stories of misguidance from clergy are all too common. They're also nothing new. The problem of brutal marital treachery has been going on for thousands of years. Untold innocent spouses have suffered savage beatings, even death at the hands of vicious covenant breakers.

No biblical study of divorce would be complete without flashing back to the final book of the Old Testament, to the well-known prophecies of Malachi on divorce. Ironically, these very words of prophecy meant to defend the innocent are routinely used against them. Some pastors and priests misquote and misapply Malachi to urge victims to stay with treacherous physical abusers.

In fairness, not all ministers of the Gospel advise tolerating this blatant kind of brutality. The majority allow divorce for victims of domestic violence. But I've heard far too many stories like the one that starts this chapter to ignore Malachi's prophetic rebuke of their priests.

Maybe you've heard the misapplied admonition that *"God hates divorce"* as often as I have. I'll admit that I took those words at face value for many years, without looking into the original language or that passage's illuminating context.

A Bit of Orientation

Though the precise date Malachi's prophecies were recorded isn't sure, it's generally accepted that they fell somewhere in the neighborhood of 450–400 B.C. Malachi's prophecies were directed at the very same problem that Mosaic Law addressed more than 800 years earlier.

By then, Israel's marital behavior had become so deplorable that, again, God chose to intervene. In righteous anger, God stepped in to prevent a greater evil that was taking place against innocent spouses. Intermarriage with idolatrous nations had become rampant and unchecked. It was also shamelessly facilitated by Hebrew leaders' favoritism toward Hebrew men.

Despite the multi-level adulteries and idolatry of the husbands and wives in Israel, notice that God directed His rebuke squarely at their priests in these opening lines of this passage on divorce:

> "*And now, this commandment is for you, O priests.* 2 *If you do not listen, and if you do not take it to heart to give honor to My name,*" *says the* LORD *of hosts, "then I will send the curse upon you...* 7 *For the lips of a priest should preserve knowledge, and men should seek instructions from his mouth; for he is the messenger of the* LORD *of hosts.* 8 *But as for you, you have turned aside from the way; you have caused many to stumble by the instruction [in the law]; you have corrupted the covenant of Levi,*" *says the* LORD *of*

> *hosts.* **9** *So I also have made you despised and abased before all the people, just as <u>you are not keeping My ways, but are showing partiality in the instruction [law]</u>.*"
>
> *Malachi 2:1–2, 7–9*

Why rebuke priests about divorce?

Does it seem strange to you that God would direct this stern rebuke at the priests? It's not that God ignored how wedded the people had become to breaking faith with one another. This was God's overarching anger that the priests were responsible for corrupting their higher covenant with Him, the priestly covenant of Levi (v. 8).

Instead of preserving the knowledge of the laws given to that point through Moses (including those on divorce), religious leaders had turned away from the law handed down from their fathers of the faith. They'd profaned the Levitical covenant. What's more, they were actively causing people to stumble by propagating false teaching. In particular, God rebuked them for showing partiality in the way they advised the people about His laws.

God condemned their bias toward the men.

This blistering reprimand serves as a direct prelude to Malachi's key passage on divorce. It gives us keen insight on just what it is God hates about divorce and why.

On both spiritual and literal planes, the priests had become woefully corrupt. They'd abandoned their priestly covenant in mercenary ways. Routinely, they allowed defiled sacrifices on His altar.

They became lax about giving sound instruction about divorce law. They favored the men who controlled the purse strings. In the process, innocent spouses suffered abominable treacheries. This prompted the Almighty to rise in defense of those innocents the priests refused to protect.

God Admonishes Judah's Treachery

Lest the men try to hide behind the robes of their wayward priests, God soundly rebuked all of Judah through Malachi:

> "*Why do we deal treacherously each against his brother so as to profane the covenant of our fathers?* **11** *Judah has dealt treacherously, and an abomination has been committed in Israel and Jerusalem; for Judah has profaned the sanctuary of the* LORD *which He loves, and has married the daughter of a foreign god.*"
>
> *Malachi 2:10b–11*

Take a close look at the original Hebrew word for treachery, *bagad*. This helps us understand the many forms such marital violations can take. The primitive root for treachery means *to cover up*. Figuratively it speaks of covert acts—pillaging, deception, desertion, and all manner of marital unfaithfulness.

The echoed Hebrew phrase used for *abomination* (*to ebah to ebah*) indicates profound abhorrence, disgusting sin, especially idolatry. The specific nature of this abomination was two-fold, like its doubled root. They had profaned God's sanctuary with defiled sacrifices, and they had wed women who served idols.

How does God punish treachery?

The penalties for treacherous abominations follow:

> "*As for the man who does this, may the* LORD *cut off from the tents of Jacob everyone who awakes and answers, or who presents an offering to the* LORD *of hosts.*"
>
> *Malachi 2:12*

This passage warns every man who commits marital treachery. It also pertains to any priest who passes biased judgments against a betrayed spouse. Together, the treacherous incur these punishments:

1) Being cut off from their people;
2) Being removed from their covering,
   their protection, their home;
3) The loss of God's regard for their tears;
4) The loss of God's favor for their offerings.

If these punishments seem overly harsh to you, remember: these are the very same treacheries the guilty have committed against their innocent spouses. In unjustly abandoning their Hebrew wives to take up with younger foreign women, guilty men have:

1) Cut their Hebrew wives off;
2) Removed their wives from their homes;
3) Become calloused to their wives' tears;
4) Refused to look upon their wives with favor.

God went on to explain exactly why He no longer accepted their defiled offerings with favor:

> *"Yet you say, 'For what reason?' Because the LORD has been a witness between you and the wife of your youth, against whom you have dealt treacherously, though she is your companion and your wife by covenant."*
>
> *Malachi 2:14*

As mentioned before, I'm sure there were times when roles were reversed, when wives betrayed their husbands, but through this particular prophecy, God specifically took treacherous men to task, citing the abominable acts of wayward priests and husbands.

Who was the wife of a man's youth?

When God referred to *the wife of your youth*, He went on to describe her as the man's *companion* and his *wife by covenant*. In so doing, God identified the original Hebrew wife that a man had wed in his youth under the Jewish covenant of marriage.

Sadly, many men sorely neglected and abandoned their Hebrew wives (just as guilty spouses do today). After their covenant wives had given them their virginity and their youth, and the best of their childbearing years, these men moved on to take younger, often idolatrous wives and lovers.

Don't forget, this prophecy applied not only to Hebrew men in general. It was specifically directed at priests who showed partiality to men, despite their covenant-breaking acts. Every time a priest unjustly favored a man, God held that priest accountable for any ills that befell the innocent spouse.

If priests didn't insist upon compliance with Mosaic Law regarding those three requirements of *provision*, *protection*, and *conjugal cohabitation*, they were partially responsible for the wife's neglect. If a priest didn't require a man to give his abandoned Hebrew wife a writ of divorce (setting her free to remarry), God held that priest partially responsible. If any harm or hardship resulted for the innocent spouse, her blood was on the priest's hands.

Why would a man avoid giving a divorce certificate?

To this day, men find reasons to abandon their wives without giving them a proper divorce. Consider this modern example:

> *"He had the soul of a poet. Though I'd known him a long time, I had no idea of his problem. Oddly, after we married, he never moved in with me. He had a place to sleep overnight at work, so I warily accepted this at first. Visits and phone contact slowed, then stopped. His creditors began to hound me. Where was his money going?*
>
> *Finally, I realized the sad truth: my absentee husband was a cocaine addict. Soon, a neighbor thwarted his attempt to rob my home while I was away. The police called, looking for him on yet another charge. Honestly, I had no idea where he*

was, even to try to get the annulment I deserved.
Heartbroken and abandoned, I filed for divorce."

Can you see why this deserter didn't stick around to assist his wife in ending their marriage? With his paycheck feeding his addiction, he was dodging creditors. The police weren't far behind. This innocent wife couldn't afford a lawyer. She was left to figure out how to divorce a man she couldn't even find.

These are the times when Christians must step up and serve as priests to one another. I'll never forget sitting with this betrayed believer, helping her complete the forms to initiate a divorce from an absentee husband. I did most of the writing because she was weeping and shaking so hard that she couldn't. God bless that dear woman. She still forgave and loved that man with all her heart, despite it all.

In Moses' day, specific issues of hardhearted stubbornness, pride, or political advantage may have played a role in why some men failed to give their wives the documentation they needed. But like that modern deserter, many Hebrew men had a financial incentive to deny giving an abandoned wife a divorce certificate.

Financial terms depended upon what was stated in each marriage certificate regarding any dowry that a woman brought into the marriage. As mentioned earlier, this served like a modern-day pre-nup.

Obtaining a proper Jewish divorce *Get* from a priest often forced repayment of the woman's dowry, especially if the wife had faithfully fulfilled her part of the marital vows.

If a man merely *put away* his wife without an official *Get*, he could avoid following through with repayment issues, since technically, he was still married to her. As for the abandoned wife, she wasn't free to remarry after being put away because—by the Letter of the Law—she was still married.

Do you see how the priests abetted some men by facilitating this treachery? Whether it meant backing a false accusation against the wife or assisting a man in depriving his wife of any rightful repayment, a priest was involved. Whenever a certificate of divorce was denied to a deserving Hebrew wife who protested, the priest sinned by turning an indifferent eye.

Like the modern battered wife opening this chapter, these abandoned women cried out to their priests. And rather than helping these innocents, the priests showed favoritism to the men, abetting their treachery against the wives of their youth.

More Controversy

Now, we come upon one of the most disputed texts in the Old Testament, the opening line of verse 15:

> "*But not one has done so who has a remnant of the Spirit. And what did that one do while he was seeking a godly offspring? Take heed then, to your spirit, and let no one deal treacherously against the wife of your youth.*"
>
> *Malachi 2:15*

As you examine various translations of the first sentence (underlined here), you'll discover that translators are poles apart about what this line actually means. You may even find an acknowledgment of this conundrum in your Bible's footnotes.

Some speculate that the original Hebrew line was corrupted by ancient scribes. They say the scribes were so uncomfortable with the line's actual meaning that they couldn't bring themselves to record it more clearly. Scribes also may have been under financial or political pressure from the priests. A scribe may have been fearful to suggest that any priest in authority over him was devoid of the Spirit. This line may also have conflicted with a scribe's personal ideology.

While many readily acknowledge the difficulty of discerning exactly what the first line of the original Hebrew means, there are those scholars who suggest that the NASB's translation that I've cited here seems most reliable. If the NASB is, in fact, most true to this prophecy's original meaning, that line has stunning implications.

In this translation, lest any guilty man try to hide behind a show of religiosity or a facade of faith, this line points out the utterly godless state of the guilty. It would mean that both priests and men who abandon their marital covenants have *no remnant of the Spirit* left at all.

It's chilling when you think about it. Clergy or not, those who act in these treacherous ways don't even have a trace of the Holy Spirit in them.

Then again, the line makes perfect sense when you realize that no one who is walking in the Spirit of God would act in such a treacherous manner against an innocent spouse. The Holy Spirit would never lead a believer to neglect, abuse, abandon, divorce, or put away his innocent wife. And a faithful priest would never condone the treachery of a man who did.

Were these men unbelievers?

Remember that while people can be swayed by outward appearances, God looks at the true state of each person's heart.

Since all genuine believers have the Holy Spirit living inside them, this translation supports that no matter what faith or religious position a person may claim, these treacherous sorts are essentially acting as unbelievers. If they ever had true faith to start with, they have denied it. In this Holy Spirit-vacated state, they are apostate wolves in sheep's clothing.

Still, in His mercy, God exhorts even these lost souls through Malachi. As the verse goes on in undisputed terms, God compels these men to take inventory of their spirits. He warns that no man should deal treacherously against the wife of his youth. God urges these men to tend to their corrupt spirits and to stop this violence against their Hebrew wives.

No matter what the correct translation of the first line in verse 15 is, one thing is clear. In God's covenant role as spiritual Husband to His Bride, God commandingly champions the cause of betrayed women in this passage. He forcefully rebukes guilty priests and unfaithful men in this valiant defense of the innocent spouse.

Immediately following that stern admonition, we find famously misquoted words. Since the underlined word is mistranslated in many Bibles, I've bracketed in a translation more consistent with the Hebrew:

> *"For I hate <u>divorce</u> [sending or putting away]," says the LORD, the God of Israel, "and him who covers his garment with wrong [or violence]," says the LORD of hosts. "So take heed to your spirit, that you do not deal treacherously."*
>
> *Malachi 2:16*

What exactly does God hate?

Let's look closely at that hot-button first line of verse 16 for the answer. First, focus on the flashpoint of controversy:

The Hebrew word is *shalach*.

Though *shalach* is often translated *divorce* (as in the NASB), the root word is more accurately defined as *to send away, put away, forsake*, or *cast out*. If your Bible translates *shalach* as *divorce*, you may even see *sending away* or *putting away* noted as preferred, alternate translations. That means this frequently quoted phrase is more faithfully translated as "*For I hate putting away*," not the oft-quoted "*For I hate [divorce]*."

What's the difference between divorce and 'putting away' again?

The distinction between divorce and putting away may not seem as stark today as it would have to Malachi's original hearers. In that day, all of Israel knew the important difference between *divorce* and *putting away*.

Again, a legal *divorce* was granted by means of a witnessed divorce certificate, fulfilling any terms of dowry repayment. This *Get* set the abandoned wife free to remarry.

If a woman were simply *put away*, that meant she was cast out of her home without a divorce *Get* and with no legal means of support. *Putting away* left her future in peril in ways a documented *divorce* didn't.

Faithfully translated, it's *putting away* that God hates. God loathes that unfair treachery of sending a faithful wife out onto the street without the freeing divorce certificate required by Mosaic Law. As the champion of the innocent spouse, God rose to the defense of every wife who was unjustly accused or denied the divorce certificate she deserved.

Yes, God hates the breaking of the marital covenant. He never wanted that. But when these men broke their vows, they bore responsibility for the dissolution of their Hebrew marriages. And God's anger erupted over the widespread treachery taking place uninhibited by priests, as men violated the marital covenant and put their innocent wives away without a proper divorce.

Notice the rest of verse one specifies where God's anger is directed in the sin of *putting away:*

> *"For I hate [putting away]," says the* LORD, *the God of Israel, "<u>and him who covers his garment with wrong [or violence]</u>," says the* LORD *of hosts. "So take heed to your spirit, that you do not deal treacherously."*

> *Malachi 2:16*

As you see, God's ire isn't leveled at the innocent spouse. It's directed squarely at *"him who covers his garment with wrong [or violence]."* So, it's the evil that comes of putting away that God says he hates in this verse. He's angered by anyone who is party to that wrongdoing and the violence involved.

God's righteous wrath is directed at:

1) **Phariseeism**
Religious legalists who show the guilty favoritism at the expense of the innocent

2) **The Faithless Spouse**
Idolaters, adulterers, neglecters, the treacherous, and the violent

This is the Spirit of the Law: God is the defender of the violated innocent spouse. His heart aches for every betrayed believer. And He went on to say that those who abuse or otherwise wrong their innocent spouses by *putting away* without a proper divorce should attend to the bankruptcy of their own spirits. They should stop their treacherous dealings.

Despite this prophetic warning, partiality toward violent spouses continues to this day. Still, many deny wrongdoing. You can just hear the vain protests of the apostate priests as God responded through Malachi in the final verse of this chapter:

"You have wearied the LORD with your words. Yet you say, 'How have we wearied Him?' In that you say, 'Everyone who does evil is good in the sight of the LORD, and He delights in them,' or, 'Where is the God of justice?' "

Malachi 2:17

The Priesthood of Believers Today

Though this prophecy was originally directed at ancient priests, we are wise if we consider the state of our own spirits. The briar patch the priests got into wasn't so different from what happens today. We let all kinds of worldly concerns sway us from taking a sound biblical course.

It gets as bad as it did in Malachi's day.

Think of a contemporary marital crisis in your life. A friend or family member may be on the verge of a break-up. You might be wrestling with what to do yourself.

Ask yourself these questions:

1) *Do I let personal sympathies tempt me to side with the guilty over the innocent?*

2) *How do I let social politics, finances, and partiality toward powerful people sway my perspective about divorce?*

3) *Have I ever rationalized unfaithfulness as okay?*

4) *How do I flirt with the boundaries of true fidelity?*

5) *Have I ever encouraged unfaithfulness in others?*

If you see yourself in any of these pitfalls, know you're not alone. We can all tire of the struggle. We feel the same pull of *situation ethics* the ancients felt.

That's why we're studying what the Bible says about divorce and remarriage. We're embracing how relevant God's Word is today, in context. We're refusing to call these Spirit-inspired words *out of touch* or *passé*. We're protecting one another from tumbling into legalism or license. We're encouraging that scriptural high road of our priestly calling.

The fact is, as believers in covenant relationship with God in Christ, we're all considered priests in His sight (1 Peter 2:9).

Whether we're facing the threat of divorce ourselves or offering advice to others, our counsel should be the same. We should reflect God's heart of justice and compassion. We should stand in defense of every innocent spouse.

•   •   •

READY TO DIVE INTO HOW JESUS addressed the great First Century divorce debate? You might be surprised at what you'll find in the next chapter.

7

First Century Debate

"I don't get it. My church teaches that the whole Bible is the inspired Word of God, including all the laws given through Moses in the Old Testament. There are certain commandments and laws they say we're still supposed to keep. Others, they say we're free of in Christ. Did Jesus cancel out Moses' divorce allowance or not?"

Despite the great value of what can be gleaned about divorce from the Old Testament, do you find some relief in moving on to the First Century and what Jesus said about divorce in the Gospels?

No matter what anyone else had to say, many see those *red-letter* words from Jesus' mouth as carrying the most weight. But as we dig into the words of our Savior, let's remember how often Jesus harkened back to the Old Testament, affirming how the Holy Spirit inspired Moses and the Prophets with God's counsel.

Keep in mind that Jesus said He came to fulfill the Law, not to abolish it—not even the smallest point of it (Matthew 5:17–18). So, let's continue to highly esteem Jesus' words in context with the entire counsel of Scripture.

There's a lot to unpack piece by piece in this chapter. But when we do, we find amazing harmony, even about emotionally charged issues like divorce and remarriage.

Schools of First Century Thought

Going from the Old Testament to the New may look like just a turn of a page in your Bible, but historically, it represents a gap of about four hundred years. When the New Testament era picked up in the First Century, a fierce debate continued to rage about divorce among the teachers of the Law. Two schools of thought dominated the conversation from late B.C. through early First Century A.D. years, based on the teachings of these two highly influential rabbis:

Hillel and Shammai.

Remember when we briefly looked at license versus legalism? Poles apart, those two stances were regularly debated by devotees of Hillel and Shammai. Anyone in First Century Palestine would have been familiar with their divorce arguments. The Pharisees would have known all about this. So would Jesus.

Hillel's 'Any Cause' Divorce

On one side, the House of Hillel promoted what was known as *any cause divorce*. Hillel cast a liberal eye on Deuteronomy 24:1's phrase for when a wife *"finds no favor"* and verse three's word for *hating* or *disliking* one's wife. Hillel plucked those words out of context and twisted them into grounds for divorce.

If you check Deuteronomy 24:1–4 in its proper context, you'll see that Moses' point was not to innumerate just causes for divorce. Instead, Moses' words were meant to prohibit remarriage to an original spouse when there had been an intervening union.

Still, Hillel took the concept of a wife not finding favor or being despised and expanded it beyond Moses' intent into very liberal grounds for divorce. He spun those out-of-context words to mean it was permitted to divorce a wife if she'd lost favor by something as simple as letting her hair down outside. Under Hillel, a man could divorce his Hebrew wife for so trivial a reason as burning his dinner.

In an effort to make these inconsequential reasons for divorce more palatable, it was rationalized that Hillel's liberal stance could help preserve the dignity and marriageability of a divorced woman. Rather than being thought of as divorced for a more serious cause that could make others hesitate to marry her, it might be assumed that she'd only made some trivial error. It might also be acknowledged that the husband had been the one to break their marital vows.

As you can imagine, Hillel's *any cause divorce* became a wildly popular view. Even after Hillel's death in 10 A.D., many embraced the easy out Hillel's school of thought encouraged, divorcing their wives for a variety of petty offenses.

Chiming in to take Hillel's *any cause divorce* to its logical extreme, Rabbi Akiva promoted *No Fault* divorce. Akiva insisted that even if a man only found another woman more likeable or attractive than his innocent Hebrew wife, he could divorce his wife to marry someone else. There would be no assigning of blame or suffering of consequences. While Hillel's view dominated, both Hillel and Akiva stood firmly in the camp of license.

Bottom line: Hillel's *any cause divorce* was easy to acquire. But it did require the husband to repay his wife's dowry as specified on the Jewish marriage certificate.

Shammai's Divorce for Sexual Immorality Only

On the flip side of the debate coin, the House of Shammai's Letter-of-the-Law teaching countered that a Hebrew wife's offense must rise to a serious level to justify divorce. Rabbi Shammai also plucked Moses' words out of context.

Shammai insisted that in the conditional verses opening Deuteronomy 24, the word Moses used for indecency (*ervah*) should be strictly interpreted to mean that sexual immorality was the only just cause for divorce.

Most say Shammai only allowed divorce on specific grounds of adultery, whereas others contend that he also allowed divorce for other forms of sexual unfaithfulness. But suffice it to say that divorces for any non-sexual reasons were considered unjust under Shammai's strict teaching.

Here's that verse Shammai referenced if you'd like to refer to it again:

> "*When a man takes a wife and marries her, and it happens that <u>she finds no favor in his eyes because he has found some indecency [ervah] in her</u>, and he writes her a certificate of divorce and puts it in her hand and sends her out from his house...*"
>
> *Deuteronomy 24:1*

Lest we jump on Shammai's bandwagon too quickly, we should first remember the multiple meanings of the Hebrew word *ervah* on which this prominent rabbi based his contention. Shammai's interpretation made divorces much harder to obtain, since a person could not divorce unless some form of sexual misconduct were charged and proven. Even if someone abandoned or attempted to murder a spouse, Shammai's teaching did not allow for divorce (because these were not sexual offenses).

Do you see how Shammai's teaching also took Moses' passage on remarriage out of context, treating it as limiting just causes for divorce? By refusing the neglect of marital covenants as legitimate grounds, Shammai used this passage to countermand a prior ruling of Mosaic Law allowing for other just causes.

Again, remember that Moses required three things of a man to remain married: *provision, protection, and conjugal cohabitation.* As we've studied, if a man hardheartedly neglected his vows to his wife in any of these three ways, Moses required him to give her a bill of divorcement, freeing her to remarry.

So, Shammai denied innocents the right of divorce (and remarriage), even though Moses considered neglect to be a just cause. Not only did Shammai take Moses out of context, he also defined Moses' word for indecency (*ervah*) less fully than the range of violations the Hebrew definition allows.

What did 'indecency' mean again?

Though we studied *ervah* in Chapter Five, let's refresh our memories on what the Hebrew word Shammai cited from Mosaic Law means.

While easily applicable to a variety of sexual sins, by definition, Moses' word e*rvah* could include an assortment of offenses. *Ervah* could mean anything from *inappropriate nudity*, some kind of *shameful behavior, a dishonorable flaw or blemish*, to some form of spiritual *uncleanness*. While *ervah's* meaning is consistent with a variety of woman's sexual sins, adultery is not listed as a meaning in any Hebrew dictionary I've found. There's a reason for that.

Don't forget the stoning penalty for adultery. Consider that in the proper context of Deuteronomy 24:1–4, Moses permitted that the wife could simply be divorced, then allowed to live and remarry. This implies that there were lesser forms of sexual immorality that also qualified as grounds for just divorce under Moses. You might also see how some significant non-sexual transgressions could have been considered biblically unclean, shameful sins, or a dishonorable defect in a person's character.

It's clear that Shammai's *only sexual immorality* stance was more limiting than Mosaic Law provided. Moses expressly permitted divorce in instances of spousal hardheartedness by serious forms of neglect.

For this reason, many deem Shammai's stance to be on the legalistic side.

Jesus Enters the Fray

Can you imagine the hotly contested debates going on between Hillel's liberal *any cause* divorce vs. Shammai's limiting *only sexual immorality* allowance? That was the veritable hornet's nest into which the Pharisees deliberately coaxed Jesus.

Since Matthew's Gospel offers some fascinating details the other Gospel writers didn't mention, we'll use Matthew's fuller account as a primary basis.

As Matthew 19 opens, we find Jesus' popularity growing by leaps and bounds. With Jesus' many miraculous signs, it's no wonder that enormous crowds flocked to His teaching. It's also no surprise that the Pharisees became jealous and attempted to undermine Jesus' influence at every turn.

In Matthew 19, once again, the teachers of the Law approached Jesus to test Him. Repeatedly, they tried to get Jesus to speak against Moses. Why? Because they wanted to trump up reasons to kill Jesus, since speaking against Moses was a capital offense in that time.

Doubtless, the Pharisees strategically constructed their question as a trap. Though the Greek word *apoluo* can mean *to divorce* or *put away*, the context of the conversation clarifies it's divorce the Pharisees probed Jesus about. Their question's phrase *any cause* would have been readily understood by hearers as a direct tie-in to the Hillel vs. Shammai divorce debate.

Those tricky Pharisees knew that to side with either Hillel's *any cause* or Shammai's *only sexual immorality* divorce could be spun as siding against Moses. Siding with Hillel could be deemed too liberal. If Jesus sided with Shammai, they could accuse Jesus of taking away from what Moses allowed.

Notice the *any cause* language of the Pharisees' question to Jesus, ripped straight from the headline of Hillel's liberal teaching:

> "*And some Pharisees came to Him, testing Him, and saying, 'Is it lawful for a man to divorce his wife for <u>any cause</u> at all?*"
>
> *Matthew 19:3*

The *any cause* detail is absent from Mark's Gospel (Mark 10:2). Thus, Matthew's account gives us an additional revealing context of this conversation to go on. In asking if divorce were lawful for *any cause*, the Pharisees essentially asked if Jesus supported Hillel's *any cause* divorce. But rather than step into their trap, Jesus was so wise. He refused to identify Himself as sitting under either Hillel's or Shammai's teaching.

Instead, both Matthew and Mark recorded that Jesus did what any truly good teacher of the Law regarding divorce should. He identified with God's ideal for marriage in Genesis.

> *"Have you not read, that He who created them from the beginning made them male and female, 5 and said, 'For this cause a man shall leave his father and mother, and shall cleave to his wife; and the two shall become one flesh'? Consequently, they are no more two, but one flesh. What therefore God has joined together, let no man separate."*
>
> *Matthew 19:4–6 (Genesis 2:24)*

Jesus took them back to the Garden of Eden. He reminded them that divorce was not ever God's intent. He stressed the spiritual nature of the one-flesh union and God's perfect will. Jesus reiterated that man and wife should cleave to each other. Then Jesus added that no one should separate what God has put together.

Did Jesus ban all divorce?

Often, Matthew 19:6 (mirrored by Mark 10:9) is interpreted as a prohibition on all divorce. That's despite Jesus' subsequent reference to Mosaic Law.

Misunderstanding Jesus' statement, some counsel innocent spouses not to be the one to file for divorce, even when in physical danger. The problem with this interpretation is that it's not consistent with the overall counsel of the Bible. That's the very definition of taking a verse out of biblical context.

What did Jesus mean?

It's that spiritual, one-flesh union—the complete integration of husband and wife—that no human being should be the first to separate. And how does that separation take place? By being the spouse who breaks a couple's marital vows. The divorce certificate Moses allowed only formalized the fact that the marital bond had already been broken.

When there are biblically just causes, to deny a betrayed believer the right to divorce doesn't even line up with the Letter of the Law, much less the Spirit of it. In calling attention to the one-flesh union that God creates through marriage, Jesus' Spirit of the Law is clear. The separation Jesus warned against is the initial sinful act that breaks the marital covenant with an innocent spouse—not the Letter of the Law divorce paperwork that Moses permitted as a result.

Just like Jesus did, there are things we should do when questioned about divorce and remarriage:

1) We should set aside human debates.

2) We should embrace the whole Bible on the subject, in its proper context.

3) We should respect God's holy ideal and keep our marriage covenants (till broken by a spouse's death or betrayal).

4) We should repent over any ways we've fallen short and ask for forgiveness.

5) We should refuse to ignore passages where the Bible allows divorce and remarriage for the sake of the betrayed, innocent spouse.

6) We should take heed to the specific instances where the Bible says divorce or remarriage would be a sin.

7) We should carefully consider if and when covenant-breaking acts have severed what God has put together and what is biblically advised in the aftermath.

8) Most of all, we should rely on the Holy Spirit's counsel in concert with the Bible.

The Pharisees' Rebuttal

When they were unable to derail Jesus over Hillel or Shammai's teaching with their first query, do you know what those scheming Pharisees did? They rewrote Moses' words of Deuteronomy 24:1 with another trick question.

Like Hillel and Shammai, the Pharisees took Moses' passage on remarriage after an intervening marriage completely out of context. Rather than accepting the divorce certificate as an element of the hypothetical situation Moses laid out, they misquoted Moses as elevating divorce into a commandment:

> "*They said to Him, 'Why then did Moses <u>command</u> to give her a certificate and divorce her?*'"
> *Matthew 19:7*

In another detail unique to Matthew's account, we observe that, immediately, Jesus saw through the trick wording of the Pharisees. Jesus corrected that Moses only *permitted* divorce, but never *commanded* it. Jesus also explained that Moses only allowed divorce "*because of your hardness of heart*" (v. 8).

Again, Jesus cited God's ideal. He reminded them that God never wanted the kind of hardheartedness that leads to divorce. But since the Fall resulted in human beings' banishment from the Garden of Eden, hardheartedness sorely compromised God's best-laid plans for marriage.

Then, Jesus redirected their attention to the proper context of Moses' if/then statements. Like Moses, Jesus spoke in conditional terms about how remarriage can lead to the sin of adultery, except when a spouse has already broken the one-flesh vow through immorality *(porneia)*.

In perfect harmony with Moses' allotment in Deuteronomy 24:1–4, Jesus mirrored Moses' context by speaking to the exception that determined if remarriage would be just or unjust:

> *"And I say to you, whoever divorces his wife, except for immorality [porneia], and marries another commits adultery [moichao]."*
>
> *Matthew 19:9*

In one sentence, Jesus drilled down to the heart of the problem that had proliferated since Moses' day. By and large, the main reason people were getting divorced was to dump a present Hebrew spouse in order to marry someone else. They were divorcing without just cause, as if that gave them license to remarry. Jesus deemed such remarriages adulterous.

Once and for all, Jesus closed the misperceived loophole such covert adulterers had been jumping through under Hillel's *any cause* divorce. Jesus exhorted that anyone who divorces a faithful spouse cannot remarry without committing the sin of adultery. No divorce certificate could be used to whitewash that sin of being the spouse who broke the marital bond.

Nowhere in this verse did Jesus prohibit the innocent spouse from having the biblical right to divorce for any legitimate cause allowed by Mosaic Law. Jesus said nothing to countermand Moses on divorce or remarriage. Rather, Jesus affirmed the divine inspiration of everything Moses recorded into Scripture, including the allowance of divorce for the sake of the innocent spouse.

Outwitting the Pharisees, Jesus only said that (except for immorality) whoever divorces his wife <u>and marries another</u> commits the sin of adultery. Just like Moses, Jesus used a multi-conditional hypothetical to make His point, pertaining when two conditions occur:

1) divorce (*except for immorality*), plus
2) remarriage to another

It wasn't divorcing a spouse that was labeled adultery in and of itself. Jesus didn't violate Moses' three requirements or say there were no other just causes for divorce. He only said that a divorcer who *remarried* after a divorce that didn't fall under the immorality exception committed and caused the sin of adultery. This is because the divorcer would be the one who unjustly broke the one-flesh bond.

In this often misunderstood and misquoted passage, Jesus plainly speaks to the core of the problem: unjust divorce to trade in one spouse and then remarry another. Unless the divorcer has already been betrayed by a spouse's breach of the one-flesh bond, that initiating divorcer cannot remarry without committing adultery.

What does this mean to the betrayed?

Forgiveness remains a scriptural imperative. Godly counsel is advised. Sincere efforts to reconcile follow God's example. But the Bible does offer ample room to believe that betrayed believers have the biblical right to divorce a spouse who has broken the marriage covenant in any of the ways Moses stated.

Jesus' debate-ending answer to the Pharisees was as compassionate toward the betrayed as it was brilliant. Take time to absorb the implications Jesus' statement has for the innocent:

> 1) If an innocent husband justly divorced his wife because she had first broken the marital covenant by immorality, Jesus set the husband free to remarry without sin.

2) If a husband divorced his wife for any reason other than her immorality, then that husband committed adultery by remarrying.

Follow the logic. In scenario number two, that husband's adultery breaks his vow to the first wife. While he must answer for his sin of adultery, if the wife were the innocent spouse in the divorce, her ex-husband's adultery justifies the betrayed first wife's remarriage all the more under Jesus' exception.

This was not the only time Jesus addressed this issue. Previous to this exchange with the Pharisees, Jesus mentioned the very same matter in his Sermon on the Mount:

> *"And it was said, 'Whoever divorces his wife, let him give her a certificate of dismissal.' But I say to you that every one who divorces his wife except for the cause of unchastity [porneia] makes her commit adultery. Again, you have heard that the ancients were told, 'You shall not make false vows, but shall fulfill your vows to the LORD.' "*
>
> *Matthew 5:31–33*

Here too, we see that blame for any adultery involved falls on the husband who divorces a faithful wife, not on the wife he causes to commit adultery. Jesus made that same exception for immorality (*porneia*), freeing whichever spouse was betrayed to remarry. Then, he topped it off with a reminder of the importance of keeping all vows made to the LORD.

No Condemnation

Did you see what's notably absent?

There is not one ounce of blame or responsibility placed upon the betrayed spouse. The unjust divorcer is at fault for committing adultery himself and for causing the betrayed spouse to remarry (thereby passively commit adultery). Those covenant-breaking sins are laid at the feet of the one who initiated the divorce to marry another person, not the innocent spouse who had to remarry to survive in that day.

In these two passages, Jesus tacitly affirmed all of Scripture, preserving Moses' allowance of divorce for just cause. Through the exception Jesus noted and His reference to the Jewish *Get*, He also allowed for remarriage for innocent victims of spousal immorality.

Case Studies

Using what you've learned thus far, evaluate these two case studies. How would you counsel each of these betrayed believers?

Kevin's wife, Ann, is caught engaging in an extramarital affair. If Ann is willing to repent and terminate the affair, is Kevin scripturally obligated to reconcile? Why or why not?

Jen's husband, Eric, has been convicted of molesting students from the gymnastics team he coaches. Does Jen have the biblical right to divorce Eric? If so, would she be free to remarry?

●　　　●　　　●

EXACTLY HOW WAS JESUS' one exception of spousal immorality defined? Perceptive question. We'll study that pivotal wording closely in the next chapter.

8

Jesus' Exception

"The last thing I ever wanted was to fall under this biblical exception. My husband's unfaithfulness drove a knife through my chest. I thought I'd never stop crying. Years later, I am still tending the wounds he inflicted on me and our family."

We must always remember: Jesus' exchange with the Pharisees was never a political debate for our Savior. Beneath Jesus' words was a heart beating for the innocent spouse, a heart that would be pierced for every human being—both perpetrators and victims of such covenant-breaking immorality.

You may have heard the immorality exception Jesus spoke of referred to as the *Matthean Exception*. While widely used by scholars, this non-biblical term can confuse the perception of authorship. Though this exception is found in Matthew's Gospel, Matthew merely recorded what Jesus said about circumstances where remarriage is permissible after divorce. So, Jesus is the one who made the exception. That's why I'll refer to immorality as *Jesus' exception* rather than Matthew's.

Why does Jesus' exception only appear in Matthew?

This question comes up a lot. Spending a little time on the authorship of the Gospels will help us embrace the reliability of Matthew's sole accounting of Jesus' exception.

Excepting immorality *(porneia)* is a detail Matthew cites twice (Matthew 5:32 and Matthew 19:9). Mark does not relate Jesus' exception in his briefer account of this event (see Mark 10:2–12). We do find the rest of essentially the same explanation from Jesus in Mark, mirroring that God never intended for marriage covenants to be broken.

As Jesus' exception is studied, questions arise about the order in which the Gospels were written (as if the first written might be deemed more reliable). Though there is some dispute about whether Matthew's or Mark's Gospel was written first, there is wide acceptance among scholars that the Gospel of Matthew is an eyewitness account, written by the Apostle Matthew. Matthew actually heard what Jesus said. Matthew's memory of this exchange helps explain why Matthew included the detail of Jesus' exception even though the other Gospels didn't.

While biblical historians consider all four of the Gospels to be accurate and reliable, neither Mark nor Luke witnessed Jesus' earthly life and ministry first-hand as Matthew and John did. Instead, as a disciple of the Apostle Peter, Mark recorded his Gospel based on Peter's eyewitness testimony. Likewise, Luke (and the Apostle Paul) gleaned from the accounts of the Apostles and likely Mary, the mother of Jesus.

Compared to Matthew and Mark, Luke touched on divorce and remarriage much more briefly. Luke 16:18 focuses on the sin of adultery that can occur in unjust remarriage.

The Apostle John recorded his eyewitness Gospel much later than the others. John didn't include Jesus' teaching on divorce at all. Though he had ample opportunity, John never contradicted what Matthew recorded in his earlier Gospel.

In closing the Gospel of John, the Apostle John acknowledged that Jesus did (and presumably said) many other things that John hadn't recorded. John 21:25 went on to suppose that if everything had been written in complete detail, "*the world itself would not contain the books which were written.*" So, we should be grateful for the additional details Matthew offers on divorce and remarriage, rather than being skeptical of them.

In writing his Gospel, it may be that Matthew's memory was jogged by some earlier documentation of Jesus' sayings (writings known as "Q") and/or anything Mark may have written. Matthew may have drawn from statements other disciples had noted or recalled. But since Matthew was the only synoptic Gospel writer who heard what Jesus said first-hand, the fact that his earliest eyewitness account is more detailed makes perfect sense. Let's not forget that Matthew's Gospel was circulated at a time when other eyewitnesses could have taken issue with anything Matthew recorded. The fact that they did not stands in silent affirmation of Matthew's account.

Still wondering why Matthew included the exception for immorality (*porneia*) that others didn't? Scholars say that Matthew was well educated and versed in the Law of Moses. Matthew was also known for speaking to the Jews.

As a tax collector, Matthew was quite accustomed to interaction with religious leadership. He would have been well aware of First Century debates on divorce and remarriage referencing Mosaic Law. So, it's no shock that this detail would have seemed important to Matthew in particular.

In the bigger picture, remember that Matthew was inspired by the Holy Spirit to include this exception twice in his Gospel. To imply that Matthew made this detail up or put this exception in of his own volition is to question the inerrancy of Scripture. The fact is, despite the great harmony of the Gospels, there are details each inspired human author mentions that others do not.

To discount what one Gospel author recorded because another didn't include it is an incredibly slippery slope. Think about it. No responsible Bible study would disregard everything that Matthew and Mark mentioned about divorce, simply because those points were not included in Luke's briefer accounting.

Rather, we examine various details unique to each Gospel. What we learn from each source contributes to a fuller array of what was said and done. Those who accept the truth and value of all Scripture embrace Jesus' immorality exception recorded by Matthew as genuine and applicable to biblical Christian living (2 Timothy 3:16).

What exactly does Jesus' immorality exception include?

By now, you may be as curious as I was about just what constituted the *immorality* Jesus cited as the exception in Matthew 19:9. Gratefully, we can check the original language for additional insight.

Jesus would have originally spoken in Hebrew, Aramaic, or possibly Greek, depending upon His hearers. Because early church writings were copied repeatedly, we don't know for certain which language Matthew chose to first record his Gospel. However, since the earliest Matthean texts we have are in Greek, we'll examine the Greek word for immorality in Matthew 19:9.

That lightning rod Greek word is *porneia.*

Though Jesus' exception is often misquoted and mistranslated as adultery (*moichao*), Matthew quotes Jesus as having used the broader Greek term— *porneia*—for this famous exception. Take another look at this verse and note the strategic positioning of these two different key words:

> "*And I say to you, whoever divorces his wife, except for immorality (porneia), and marries another commits adultery (moichao).*"
>
> *Matthew 19:9*

There are important distinctions between the two Greek words: *porneia* and *moichao.* Whereas *moichao* is defined as the particular sin of adultery, *porneia* is an umbrella word covering various ways infidelity can manifest. This makes Jesus' exception applicable to a variety of covenant-breaking "adulteries." Your Bible may translate *porneia* as another form of sexual immorality from this exception's list of legitimate meanings. There is the tendency to trust whichever translation we favor. But when the root word has multiple meanings, it's very helpful to go back to the original language from which all translators drew.

Porneia is a Greek feminine noun, referring to any of a number of forms the covenant-breaking offense of unfaithfulness can take. Under each main definition heading, I've listed underlying types of infidelity that may violate the marriage covenant. Some are modern.

Keep in mind that while none of these immoral acts are to be taken lightly, they represent the Letter of the Law. The overarching Spirit of the Law of Christ is that grace covers a multitude of sins.

Though all these sins represent hardheartedness, it would be equally hardhearted to stretch this text beyond its intent in order to wiggle out of unwanted marriage bonds. Things like a non-sexual flirtation, or an isolated slip into a lesser immorality should be addressed by confession, repentance, and counseling. Forgiveness should not be withheld.

Let's be clear that sins on this list should never be taken into trivial extremes, and then spun as legitimate biblical grounds for divorce. With that disclaimer firmly in mind, consider this word study of what *porneia* may include:

PORNEIA MEANINGS:

Harlotry, fornication, sexual immorality, idolatry (figuratively).

Harlotry

Buying, selling, and/or taking part in extramarital sexual activities such as prostitution, electronically communicated whoredom for hire (such as brokering or participating in phone or Internet sexuality); pornographic posing or performance, sexually-explicit acts for pay or professional advancement;

Fornication

Consenting sexual acts between unmarried persons (with one or more partners); may involve various acts of sexual immorality as below;

Sexual Immorality

Consenting sexual acts outside of biblical marriage (*inclusive of sexual foreplay, copulation, visual, aural, oral, and manual stimulation, manipulation, gratification leading toward and including sexual intercourse*), adultery (*sexually charged participation in an extramarital relationship—whether verbal, written, graphic, emotional, or physical*); incest, pedophilia, bestiality; perpetration of rape, molestation, sexual abuse; promiscuity, indecent exposure, willful sexually provocative extramarital nudity; unrepentant habitual sexual stimulation and/or gratification by means of pornography; unchastity, unfaithfulness;

Idolatry (figuratively) (*See 1 Corinthians 7:12–13*)
Spiritual adultery or unfaithfulness; consultation of or taking part in emotional, physical, sensual, mental, or spiritual acts of attendance, subjection, worship, reverence, and/or devotion directed toward any being, object, or ideology outside of the expressed biblical dictates of covenant relationship with God.

No doubt, Jesus' exception for *porneia* covers a lot of serious immoral ground. Adultery is often thought of as the sole exception Jesus made. It's certainly a common form of sexual infidelity. But clearly there are various related types of adulteries that may be considered under the exception of Matthew 19:9, allowing for innocents to divorce and remarry.

What all facets of *porneia* have in common is the breaking of a covenant relationship by devoting one's self to another, outside the one-flesh covenant that a husband and wife have made with God.

A Word about Pornography

As you can see, most definitions refer to some sort of sexual sin against a spouse. You may recognize *porneia* as the root of the English word *pornography*, a graphic form of sexual immorality and unfaithfulness where a spouse finds sexual stimulation or gratification by lusting over explicit images of a non-spouse.

We won't take time to address the many other forms of sexual immorality, but given the escalating pornography problem within the church, perhaps a quick caution is in order. Use of pornography is a forgivable sin, but the damage it does to the one-flesh bond of marriage is not to be underestimated.

Lest we lull ourselves into believing that marital unfaithfulness via pornography doesn't rise to the level of covenant-breaking sexual immorality, consider Jesus' prelude to His words about divorce in the Sermon on the Mount:

> *"You have heard it said, 'You shall not commit adultery;'* **28** *but I say to you, that every one who looks on a woman to lust for her has committed adultery with her already in his heart."*
>
> *Matthew 5:27–28*

This verse clearly applies to pornography. Jesus took adultery of the heart very seriously. So should we. With the proliferation of electronic pornography, temptation lurks constantly, coaxing believers into indulging their eyes, ears, and fantasies in secret.

Christians, guard your hearts against all forms of extramarital sensuality. No matter what form is a temptation for you, here are some things you can do:

1) Ask God to forgive you and set you free from the prison of that sin.

2) Cut off every access that threatens the sanctity of your marriage. Install filters with passwords unknown by you.

3) See the allures of sexual immorality as the insidious enemy traps that they are.

4) Confess this besetting sin to a Christian confidant. Make yourself accountable to godly counsel and a recovery group.

5) Recommit yourself to be wholly faithful to your spouse.

Why is idolatry a form of porneia?

The host of sexual sins under *porneia's* immoralities notwithstanding, the inclusion of idolatry as a definition for *porneia* is striking, isn't it? You may have been as surprised to see idolatry on that list as I was at first. But the more I considered this, the more sense it made.

Repeatedly, the Old Testament uses *porneia's* Hebrew equivalent, *taznuth*, to refer to the spiritual harlotries of idolatry. It speaks of the same kind of spiritual unfaithfulness for which God justly divorced Israel.

Because devotees to false gods can be readily identified as unbelievers, there's plenty of biblical room to consider that Jesus' exception (allowing for just remarriage) also applied to those worshiping idols. This aspect of Jesus' exception must still be weighed in concert with Paul's counsel to stay with unbelievers who are content to remain married to believers (See 1 Corinthians 7:12–13).

We'll study Paul's directives for those married to unbelievers in depth later. But since idolatry is a legitimate aspect of immorality (*porneia*), it does seem to indicate that Jesus allowed for a believer to remarry after being abandoned by an unbelieving idolater, just as Moses and the Prophets did.

For believers, God is an essential party to the marriage vows we make. Idolatry breaks the intimate, covenant oneness with God just as surely as adultery does. Remember, when God (as spiritual Husband) divorced Israel (His Bride), He referred to His just grounds interchangeably as adultery, harlotry, and idolatry. That helps us understand why idolatry is considered figurative adultery under Jesus' exception.

With the use of the word *porneia*, the full range of that word's meanings are concisely excepted in Matthew 19:9. Jesus made God's ideal of cleaving in faithful covenant marriage clear. He exhorted against human hardheartedness that breaks vows and leads to divorce. Then, with Jesus' one dense-packed word, the right of all innocent victims of *porneia* to divorce and remarry was affirmed. This pops off the pages of the Bible and resonates with modern-day application.

> *"When I confronted my wife about the affair she was having with a wealthy married man, she refused to end it. Instead, she asked for an open marriage. Primarily, she'd be with her lover, but she wanted to keep me on the hook in case things didn't work out. Even as inactive as I was in my faith at that point, I still knew what she wanted was completely wrong. I filed for the divorce, but her infidelity gave me just cause. Five years later, my relationship with God began to grow. Happily, I met a wonderfully faithful Christian woman and made her my bride."*

There are times when life seems like it couldn't be worse for the innocent spouse. There are those devastating betrayals to weather. Sometimes it can take years to recover from those wounds the guilty inflict—longer still to rebuild trust.

But thank God for the healing and redemption that can occur in Christ. What grace it is that the innocent spouse can turn to a God who cares, who knows the pain of betrayal personally.

Jesus and Moses in Accord

There are those who see Jesus as changing the Law of Moses in Matthew 19:9. But it's important to track how Jesus referred to Moses earlier in Matthew's Gospel. In addressing this still current-day issue, Jesus didn't nullify what Moses said. Rather, He fulfilled and clarified the Spirit of Mosaic Law.

> *"Do not think that I came to abolish the Law or the Prophets; I did not come to abolish, but to fulfill."*
>
> Matthew 5:17

The Greek for fulfill (*pleroo*) sheds light on Jesus' intent. Literally, *pleroo* means to level up, to fill in any hollows of correct understanding. Where there were any misperceived loopholes, Jesus closed them. Figuratively, it's as if Jesus said he came to satisfy the Law—to coincide with, to affirm, and execute everything Moses and the Prophets said before Him.

Consider Matthew's record of the transfiguration of Jesus in Matthew 17:1–3, when Jesus spoke with Moses and Elijah, face to face. We don't know what they talked about, but the picture Matthew painted is one of heavenly accord.

Jesus sided neither with the license of Hillel nor the legalism of Shammai. Jesus sided only with the inspired Word of God through Moses. Jesus relieved all doubt about what Moses said by filling in the hollows of Moses' directive.

Notice how deftly Jesus brought Moses' Law into present day application in Matthew 19:8. Instead of referring to Israel's ancestors by saying Moses permitted *them* to divorce for *their* hardness of heart, Jesus said, "Because of *your* hardness of heart, Moses permitted *you* to divorce *your* wives."

Jesus did not contradict Moses or take away the right to just-cause divorce Moses provided for the innocent spouse. He didn't call obtaining the certificate for just-cause divorce a sin in and of itself. Rather, Jesus called the divorcer's remarriage a sin, except when divorcing for immorality (*porneia*).

When the guilty spouse broke faith by *porneia*, the marriage covenant could be dissolved without sin by—and for the sake of—the innocent spouse. Everyone in Jesus' hearing would have been familiar with the Jewish divorce certificate's specific language and purpose, freeing the innocent spouse from all marital bonds and permitting remarriage.

Jesus knew the hardheartedness that persisted in their hearts. He knew that—just like today—most who tried to get out of a marriage did so to unjustly remarry. So He made it clear that anyone who remarried unjustly would be guilty of adultery, an abomination still punishable by stoning at that time.

Why is adultery an abomination?

Marriage is the melding of both the physical and spiritual aspects of human beings. This ties our holy God into the one-flesh union:

> "*Do you not know that your bodies are members of Christ? Shall I then take away the members of Christ and make them members of a harlot? May it never be!* **16** *Or do you not know that the one who joins himself to a harlot is one body with her? For He says, 'The two will become one flesh.'* **17** *But the one who joins himself to the* LORD *is one spirit with Him.* **18** *Flee immorality. Every other sin that a man commits is outside the body, but the immoral man sins against his own body.* **19** *Or do you not know that your body is a temple of the Holy Spirit who is in you, whom you have from God, and that you are not your own?* **20** *For you have been bought with a price: therefore glorify God in your body.*"
>
> *1 Corinthians 6:15–20*

Adultery destroys the intimacy of a believer's union with Christ at its very core. It is spiritual betrayal, devastatingly destructive.

Consider the following wisdom from the book of Proverbs:

> *"The one who commits adultery with a woman is lacking in sense [or heart]; he who would destroy himself [his soul] does it."*
>
> *Proverbs 6:32*

Jesus puts those who reason that adultery isn't a big deal on notice. He knows the deepest secrets of our hearts. He sees our true motives. Just look at this warning from Revelation:

> *"Behold, I will cast her upon a bed of sickness, and those who commit adultery with her into great tribulation, unless they repent of her deeds...**23** I am He who searches the minds and hearts; and I will give to each of you according to your deeds."*
>
> *Revelation 2:22–23*

Adultery is akin to idolatry as it bows down to the enemy to indulge fleshly desire, exposing our pure relationship with God to a sin that He condemns (Hebrews 13:4).

What about reconciliation?

Still, questions linger. Though believers are always to forgive, must an innocent spouse reconcile after a mate's sexual immorality is discovered? Or does the innocent have the scriptural right to pursue divorce immediately?

Theologians differ on this question. Some argue that the innocent should always attempt reconciliation if the vow-breaker is repentant and willing to recommit to faithfulness. Others reason that the innocent spouse is freed when the marriage covenant has been broken. Thus, the innocent spouse has the unfettered biblical option to create a new covenant with a forgiven spouse or to pursue divorce at will.

It may be hard to imagine how trust could be rebuilt after marital betrayal. But then again, God set the example. God demonstrated great grace by extending the hand of reconciliation after He divorced Israel. Hosea echoes this ideal. Moses only forbids reconciliation with an original spouse after an intervening marriage. While Jesus urges forgiveness, He also affirms the Law and the Prophets, including the right of divorce and remarriage Moses permitted for the sake of the innocent spouse.

Scripture is far from silent on this issue. As we continue to consider divorce and remarriage in light of the whole Bible, let's refrain from becoming too strident about one route where an alternative is biblically allowed. Let's give the offended party the same liberty God does, to carry out his or her own decision in faith.

Discussion Questions

1) *What were the two major sides in the divorce debate in the First Century? How did Jesus' teaching differ?*

2) *What covenant-breaking sins fall under Jesus' immorality (porneia) exception?*

3) *Has my understanding about what Jesus said about divorce and remarriage changed in any way? If so, how?*

•   •   •

DO YOU HAVE TROUBLE sorting out Paul's teaching on divorce and remarriage? Let's explore that together in the next chapter.

9

Pauline Counsel

"I never saw it coming. The day started like any other. Then, it was like whiplash. One moment I felt reasonably secure in my marriage, and the next, I'd been deserted by my unbelieving spouse. Compounding the betrayal, he left me for someone I knew, someone that I'd considered a friend."

Some things haven't changed in thousands of years. The ravages of marital betrayal ache like nothing else. Husbands and wives still abandon one another, leaving devastated innocent spouses to sort through the rubble and rebuild their shattered lives.

Flashing back to the First Century, we find Paul's letters to the early church, addressing issues just like this: marriage, divorce, and remarriage.

Like Jesus did, Paul affirmed Moses and the Prophets. In so doing, Paul implicitly incorporated everything that had been said by them before him. And he reveled at how all of Scripture furnished believers with every instruction needed for life and godliness (2 Timothy 3:14–17).

For example, consider an excerpt from Paul's letter to the church in Rome. Paul prefaced his point by saying he was speaking to those who knew the Law. In context, his overall aim wasn't to offer instruction about earthly divorce or remarriage. Rather, he was using an example from marriage to establish that the Law's jurisdiction over a person was lifelong.

> *"For the married woman is bound by the law to her husband while he is living; but if her husband dies, she is released from the law concerning her husband. 3 So then if, while her husband is living, she is joined to another man, she shall be called an adulteress; but if her husband dies, she is free from the law, so that she is not an adulteress, though she is joined to another man. 4 Therefore, my brethren, you were also made to die to the Law through the body of Christ, that you might be joined to another, to Him who was raised from the dead, that we might bear fruit for God."*
>
> *Romans 7:2–4*

As we examine Paul's framework, we see that he was only using human marriage as a metaphor to support his main contention. Paul was trying to help believers understand how they had died to their Old Covenant (the Law) and were thereby released to live in the New Covenant as the Bride of the risen Christ.

There are those who use these verses from Romans to insist that a woman should never divorce her husband. They cite this brief comparison, as if it cancels out all other biblical exceptions made by Paul's predecessors, as well as Paul's own allowances made in his letter to the Corinthians. To do this is to take Paul's words out of context, both with the perspective of Romans 7 and the entire Bible.

Everything Paul said about marriage in his brief comparison is consistent with the Scriptures. It's just that these words only represent part of the total picture. Paul didn't elaborate on exceptions with which his First Century readers were already well familiar. How do we know they were familiar? Because Paul opened this passage by saying:

"For I am speaking to those who know the law."
Romans 7:1

Even though the lifelong marriage covenant only exemplified Paul's point, there is still wisdom to be gleaned from his short comparison. A wife should

147

never divorce her faithful husband in order to marry another man.

Any wife who would initiate divorce without valid biblical grounds would never be considered the innocent spouse. Exceptions from Moses and Jesus would only apply if the husband were unfaithful to his vows in some scriptural manner, giving his innocent wife just cause to divorce him.

Women as Divorce Initiators

There's another interesting bit of sociological data Paul's verses in Romans reveal. Whereas only men could divorce their wives in Moses' day, Paul's words give us a peek into accepted Jewish norms of the First Century. By then, wives had the right to initiate divorce, too.

With the debate between Hillel's *any cause divorce* still so popular, wives could sin by citing trivial grounds for divorce just as readily as their husbands. As you can imagine, the proliferation of unjust divorce and remarriage posed a significant problem within the growing church.

As a side note: though a small minority view holds that the Bible only allows men to divorce their wives, Paul's acceptance that women also had the right to initiate divorce reads between the lines of his letters. Clearly, Paul didn't encourage unjust divorce for believers of either gender. To the contrary, Paul taught believers to remain faithful to their marriage vows. In keeping with the inspired Word of God before him, Paul urged reconciliation when possible.

But the very fact that Paul never specifically countered the accepted First Century Jewish norm of a woman's right to a just divorce is telling. This syncs well with Paul's teaching that because we're no longer under the Law, there is neither male nor female, since we are all one in Christ (Galatians 3:24–28).

As New Covenant believers, men and women have the same scriptural mandate to remain faithful to their marriage vows. Both genders are equally urged to reconcile marital estrangements where possible. And tragically, when a guilty spouse irreconcilably breaks marital faith with an innocent man or woman, the betrayed are equally permitted to seek biblical divorce for just cause.

Corinthian Counsel

Paul's acceptance of a woman's identical standing in divorce also shows in the interchangeable language of his lengthier instructions on divorce, found in his letter to the Corinthians. Notice how equally Paul mirrored his exhortation between men and women as we dive into these next two passages. In doing so, Paul made it clear that whatever he said about wives was applicable to husbands. First, Paul addressed "*the married.*" Since no unfaithfulness is mentioned, this applies to those whose covenant vows have been kept by both spouses thus far:

> "*But to the married I give instructions, not I, but the* LORD, *that the wife should not leave her husband* **11** *(but if she does leave, let her remain unmarried, or else be reconciled to her husband), and that the husband should not send his wife away [or leave his wife].*"
>
> *1 Corinthians 7:10–11*

Note Paul's emphasis that "*the married*" were to receive this as coming from *the* LORD, rather than from himself. Prophetically, Paul instructed all those in faithful marriages to stay that way. Those who do leave an innocent spouse are to remain unmarried or seek reconciliation. This encourages fidelity. It closes alternate marital doors for anyone who would unjustly desert a faithful spouse. All believers who depart without just cause are biblically compelled to return to their innocent spouses.

Like Jesus' words in Matthew 5:32 and 19:9, Paul's exhortation is directed at those who would abandon their vows, rather than at the faithful spouse.

As we read this in line with what Moses and Jesus said, we understand that this passage is not meant to prohibit just-cause divorce for innocent victims of betrayal. Again, like Jesus, Paul didn't address the innocent in verse 11. Rather, Paul entreated all unjustly departing spouses to remain true to their faithful spouses, as long as that spouse lives.

If a Believing Spouse Leaves

Paul made it clear that the directive to reconcile still applies post-divorce by saying the [unjustly] departing spouse should remain *"unmarried." Unmarried* status isn't conferred until a legal divorce has been granted. Therefore, Paul's instruction that the divorcer should reconcile persists even after an unjust divorce.

But is the unjustly deserted spouse obligated to reconcile? Some reason that innocents are released immediately to rebuild their lives. After all, the divorce certificate Moses permitted freed innocents to remarry. However, the Spirit of Paul's teaching seems to indicate that deserted innocents are encouraged to accommodate reconciliation. Particularly if the one-flesh bond hasn't been broken by the deserter's adultery, innocents can allow time for a departed spouse to return. They can make themselves available to reconciliation efforts Paul urges deserters to make.

Though Paul didn't enumerate just causes or exceptions from Moses, the Prophets, or Jesus, Paul's ardent support of their teachings makes their inclusion implicit. These words Paul attributed to the LORD are no more contradictory with Moses' or Jesus' exceptions than they are with the exception Paul cited later in this passage. So, we read Paul's points in conjunction with the overall prophetic counsel of Scripture.

Respectfully, when we parenthetically remind ourselves of exceptions and details gleaned from other biblical verses on divorce and remarriage, Paul's counsel might read something like this:

> *"But to the married I give instructions, not I, but the LORD, that the wife should not leave her husband [without biblically just cause]* **11** *but if she does leave [without biblically just cause], let her remain unmarried [except if leaving for the just cause of the other's immorality/porneia, in which case the innocent spouse may remarry without committing adultery], or else be reconciled to her husband [unless there has been an intervening marriage], and that the husband should not [leave or] send his wife away [except if the spouse is an unbeliever who chooses to leave the believer, in which case, the believer is unbound].*
>
> *1 Corinthians 7:10–11*

Can you see why Paul just let things that were biblically implicit go unrepeated here? The structure of these verses gets very convoluted by repeatedly adding in the exceptions cited elsewhere in Scripture. Whenever we read verses like this that other verses speak to, we should consider them in agreement with all other verses that have bearing.

Even after such partings occur, the one-flesh bond remains until one spouse or the other breaks it with another person. In that event, responsibility for any adultery involved is borne by the unjust divorcer (whose breach put the innocent in a position to remarry). The innocent spouse is thereby exonerated under Jesus' immorality exception.

What God said vs. what Paul said

As Paul forged onward into verse 12, he framed the next part as his personal conviction. Instead of saying this point was from the LORD (as he wrote that his prior point was), he positions verses 12–15 as his own considered advice.

Paul didn't expound upon why he specified where certain points of counsel were coming from in this chapter. He may have just wanted to be frank about what he was sure came to him prophetically as opposed to being generated in his own renewed mind.

We should also briefly consider that this may have had to do with the fact that Paul addressed this letter to the budding Gentile church in Corinth.

Behind the First Century Scenes

If we check Acts 15:1–31, it gives us a peek into context. Jewish believers sincerely wrestled with how much, if any, of the Law they should encourage Gentile believers to observe.

After Paul and Barnabas related the miracles God was doing among the Gentiles to the Apostles in Jerusalem, it was James who proclaimed in the Spirit that they should not trouble the Gentiles with observing the great body of Law from which Christ had freed them. They were simply to instruct the Gentiles to abstain from the pollution of idols, blood, things strangled, and from immorality (*porneia*).

Paul knew the Law's prohibition for marrying outside the faith (Deuteronomy 7:3–4). He was well schooled in how mixed-faith marriages could draw believers into the idolatry of their unbelieving spouses (Exodus 34:12–16). Paul respected Ezra's directive that God's people should put away their idolatrous wives. So, Paul proceeded with caution when advising Gentiles within the purview of the Jews. It could be why he attributed certain things to himself.

Handling Mixed-Faith Marriages

It's fair to assume that many Gentiles were married before they came to Christ. Suddenly, those whose spouses didn't believe were in mixed-faith marriages. Would advising these Gentiles to divorce unbelieving spouses be too much for the tender beginnings of their faith to bear? Would those who sought Paul's life use anything he said about this against him, as if he disrespected Ezra or Mosaic Law?

As we pick up where we left off, we see the wise counsel Paul gave, carefully prefacing it as from his own reasoning, thereby avoiding conflict with those who had spoken for the LORD before him:

> "*But to the rest I say, not the LORD, that if any brother has a wife who is an <u>unbeliever</u> [apistos], and she consents to live with him, let him not send her away [or leave her].* **13** *And a woman who has an unbelieving husband, and he consents to live with her, let her not send her husband away [or leave her husband].*"
>
> *1 Corinthians 7:12–13*

While Paul's personal admonition to the Gentiles set a New Covenant precedent, it still respected those who were of the conviction to observe the prophetic counsel of the Law. It also harmonized with Jesus' teaching on the divine institution of marriage, binding spouses in one-flesh union.

Going forward in Christ, Paul urged those believers who unwittingly found themselves married to unbelievers not to unjustly leave or send away an unbelieving spouse—not if the unbeliever consented to stay in the marriage. If the unbeliever were content to remain in a mixed-faith marriage, Paul directed the believer to stay with godly purpose:

> *"For how do you know, O wife, whether you will save your husband? Or how do you know, O husband, whether you will save your wife?"*
> *1 Corinthians 7:16*

This is not to say that the believer should subject the unbelieving spouse to inordinate pressure. Peter's observation to wives can also be applied to husbands as the married live in mutual submission (Ephesians 5:21). Believing spouses should let the testimony of their regenerated lives do most of the talking:

> *"In the same way [as Jesus], you wives, be submissive to your own husbands so that if any of them are disobedient to the Word they may be won without a word by the behavior of their wives, 2 as they observe your chaste and respectful behavior."*
> *1 Peter 3:1–2*

Define Unbeliever

With so many wolves in sheep's clothing out there, how do we know exactly what Paul meant when he called a person an unbeliever? First, we turn to this letter's original language.

The Greek word Paul used for *unbeliever* is *apistos*. Actively, *apistos* refers to a disbelieving individual, someone without Christian faith, a heathen. These are those who neither profess nor live as followers of Jesus. Passively, *apistos* also refers to those whose actions consistently demonstrate that they have abandoned any faith they claim. This includes any unfaithful, untrustworthy vow-breaker, or infidel. Practical unbelievers may claim to believe, but their lives bear the bitter fruit of unbelief.

Jesus wasn't shy about identifying these practical unbelievers, even those among religious leadership. He reminded us that we can discern true believers from those who only say they believe by examining their fruit. Despite the many words a person may speak in Jesus' name, Jesus said only those who do the will of His Father are true believers. Lawless workers of iniquity are all practical unbelievers (Matthew 7:15–23).

In his Epistle, James concurs. James explains the deadness of a "faith" that doesn't bear good fruit. And as to those who merely say they believe?

> *"You believe that God is one. You do well; the demons also believe and shudder."*
>
> *James 2:19*

Clearly, intellectual and/or verbal assent does not qualify a human being as a believer any more than it does a demon. Church membership, religious titles, and claims mean nothing if they are not evidenced by the godly fruit of true faith.

Paul enumerates the fruit of the flesh in his letter to the Galatians. Some additional definitions based on Paul's root Greek words are bracketed in below:

> *"Now the deeds of the flesh are evident, which are: immorality [adultery], impurity [extramarital sex], sensuality, **20** idolatry, sorcery [mediation with the dead, witchcraft], enmities [hatred, hostility], strife, jealousy, outbursts of anger, disputes, dissensions, factions [putting forth heresies], **21** envyings, [murder], drunkenness, carousings [rioting], and things like these, of which I forewarn you just as I have forewarned you that those who practice such things shall not inherit the kingdom of God."*
>
> *Galatians 5:19–21*

Note that in verse 21, Paul ends this list with a chilling warning: *those who practice such things shall not inherit the kingdom of God.*

It's not that an occasional outburst of anger or bout of envy makes a spouse an unbeliever. We all fall short in some of these ways from time to time. And we should forgive one another just as we've been forgiven (Ephesians 4:32). Rather, Paul is talking about those who unrepentantly practice these fleshly fruits as their regular mode of life. Their bad fruit, developed over time, evidences that they are unbelievers, no matter what faith they may claim.

In contrast, Paul follows with the fruit that a true Christian will bear, evidencing the active presence of the Holy Spirit, who lives in all genuine believers:

> *"But the fruit of the Spirit is love, joy, peace, patience, kindness, goodness, faithfulness, gentleness, self-control; against such things there is no law."*
>
> *Galatians 5:22–23*

Faithfulness vs. Unfaithfulness

Notice that faithfulness is among the good fruit believers should bear. Spousal faithfulness applies to all aspects of the marital covenant. This includes Moses' three requirements of provision, protection, and conjugal cohabitation.

Faithfulness should manifest not only physically, but also on practical levels, such as using one's best efforts to provide reasonable financial support and routine maintenance for the household. Provision of protection, and one's physical presence (to love, cherish, and keep) implicitly underlie each of these manifestations of faithfulness.

Most usually associate unfaithfulness with adultery, but there is more than one way to be guilty of marital unfaithfulness. Meaningful violations of the marriage vow of faithfulness are serious biblical breaches. Paul says those who commit them have denied the faith, that they are even worse than unbelievers.

Consider Paul's definition of an unbeliever in conjunction with what he wrote in his letter to Timothy:

> *"But if any one does not provide for his own, and especially for those of his own household, he has denied [disavowed, rejected] the faith, and is worse than an unbeliever [infidel]."*
>
> *I Timothy 5:8*

What if a spouse can't provide?

No inadvertent failure or unintended inability of a spouse to provide for Moses' requirements makes a spouse equal to an unbeliever. In this present, challenging economy—with joblessness on the rise—a spouse's best efforts to find gainful employment and provide are to be deemed faithful. The good faith expressed by a spouse's best efforts should be appreciated and credited as righteousness.

Hard times should be weathered together as part of the *"for better or worse"* vows. If a spouse cannot provide conjugal relations because of injury, disease, or impotence, that falls under the grace of *"in sickness and in health."* It wouldn't be right to consider a spouse deployed on military duty unfaithful, simply because the job requires time away.

What is fair to expect are sincere, best efforts on all counts. There are many ways an unemployed or disabled spouse can faithfully compensate through acts of love and service. Only willful, neglectful failure to provide rises to the level of biblical unfaithfulness equating to unbelief.

In the end, no matter what spouses may say they believe or don't, Paul's word *apistos* refers to those who live out an unbelieving state of spirit. This includes those who have never come to saving faith in Christ. It also encompasses apostates who may have once believed, but who have abandoned what faith they once had, either as a belief system or in regular practice.

It's an unsettling truth that *apistos* does not always refer to the unconverted. Jesus used the same word to exhort Thomas in John 20:27. So, why did Paul advise believers to stay in such unequally yoked marriages?

> *"For the unbelieving husband is sanctified through his wife, and the unbelieving wife is sanctified through her believing husband; for otherwise your children are unclean, but now they are holy."*
>
> *1 Corinthians 7:14*

Out of context, this verse can cause a lot of confusion. But in harmony with the entire counsel of Scripture and in the perspective of its time, we find greater clarity.

Let's start by clearing the decks of what Paul did not mean. Coming to saving faith is an individual choice that Paul later suggests that the believer may yet help lead the unbeliever to make. So, salvation via marriage cannot be what Paul intended to convey in verse 14. It's not like marrying a believer makes an unbeliever an automatic citizen of heaven.

While a godly spouse can set the example of faith, no believer can make that choice for a spouse or any child. Each and every man, woman, and child must ultimately embrace or reject Christian faith for themselves.

No one marries into salvation.

If Paul didn't mean that marriage to a believer saved a spouse or children, what did Paul mean about them being sanctified by being married to a believer? For thousands of years, only unions between those of the Jewish faith were considered legitimate marriages under God. Marriages outside the Jewish faith were not considered valid.

As married Gentiles entered the household of faith in Christ, some already married to one another, and some intermarrying with Jews, burning questions quickly arose:

- *Were Gentile marriages recognized as lawful?*
- *Could Jewish and Gentile believers intermarry?*
- *Should believers abandon unbelieving spouses?*
- *Would their children be considered legitimate?*

You can imagine the grenade it would have thrown into the homes of the fledgling Gentile church if Paul had declared their marriages invalid and directed them to divorce any unbelieving spouses. Instead, like Jesus, Paul chose his words wisely when addressing matters of Mosaic Law. He spoke in figurative language that the people of that time understood.

By saying an unbeliever is *sanctified* by a believing spouse, Paul declared those mixed-faith marriages valid under God. He deemed all children of such a marriage legitimate. It was not that the unbeliever or any children were thought to have saving faith.

Rather, the faith of the believer was accepted as enough to sanctify his or her household as a qualified lawful and binding marriage under God's blessing and covenant. Paul's three-fold message to believers married to unbelievers in Corinth was clear:

1) Stay married (if your spouse consents).
2) Your marriage is legally valid and binding.
3) Any children you have are legitimate.

Paul said nothing to countermand the directive to marry only within the faith going forward. But think what a relief this letter must have been to loving Gentile families who'd married before one spouse came to faith. Finally, their unions were recognized within the church as lawfully sanctified marriages.

What about those who are deserted by unbelievers?

Paul went on to offer relief and consolation for the innocent abandoned spouse:

> *"Yet if the unbelieving one leaves, let him leave; the brother or the sister is not under bondage in such cases, but God has called us to peace."*
>
> 1 Corinthians 7:15

In one verse, Paul set believers free from marriage vows an unbeliever abandoned. This tracks perfectly with Moses' directives when a spouse failed to meet the three requirements of provision, protection, and conjugal cohabitation. Just as an abandoned wife was entitled to a divorce certificate in cases of neglect (including failure to cohabitate), so were deserted innocent spouses.

Over the course of marriage to a believer, the unbeliever has ample opportunity to consider Christ's call on his or her life. In leaving, the unbeliever rejects both the believer and God's grace. If the deserter hasn't already committed adultery, in many cases it's not long before that one-flesh bond is also broken.

Scriptural grounds for letting an unbeliever go without attempts to reconcile also come from this passage. Following the unbeliever's departure, the innocent spouse may file for a just-cause divorce immediately, without sin. The believer is released from all bonds of the marriage covenant that the unbeliever has broken by desertion.

When believers marry unbelievers

Those who knowingly marry unbelievers in the hope of leading them to saving faith in Christ often find themselves in bewildering predicaments.

"In a way, it's my own fault that I'm in this mess. I tried so hard to lead my spouse to Jesus, but instead he devoted himself to an insatiable gambling addiction. I made the worst mistake of my life when I married an unbeliever. Now I'm paying the consequences for my own sin of disobedience. Will God still help me?"

The answer to this humbly repentant believer is a resounding *yes!* Though we should never knowingly rely on God's grace when disregarding the Bible's instruction to marry only within our faith, our God is full of lavish mercy and forgiveness. In time, this unbelieving spouse's adultery and desertion set his innocent spouse free from the vows he had broken. It hasn't been easy, but day-by-day, God is helping her rebuild her life.

Wonder why we've spent so much time defining the scriptural difference between marriage to a true believer and an unbeliever? It's time well spent since the Bible's directives to believers differ between these two spiritual statuses.

Case Studies

Are you ready to exercise what we've learned in some practical case studies? What biblical counsel would you offer to the innocent spouses in the following scenarios?

James realized he was sterile just weeks after marrying his believing wife, Liz. Liz has always wanted children of her own. Since James can't father children, Liz wants an annulment. She reasons that she must give herself time to find someone else while she's young enough to bear children. Should James attempt to reconcile with Liz or should he let her go?

Caroline becomes an astrologist after marrying Duncan. She is content to remain married to Duncan, but Duncan is uncomfortable with her zodiac paraphernalia and the readings she does for her friends and clients. Does Duncan have biblical grounds to divorce Caroline if she insists upon her right to practice astrology in their home?

Traci's husband, Jack, was baptized as a child, but never pursued a relationship with God as an adult. He'd much rather play poker and prowl sports bars with his buddies than go to church with Traci. Tired of petty squabbles over their incompatible lifestyles, Jack moves into a separate apartment where he can be himself. What are Traci's biblical obligations to Jack, if any?

Do you see how real life conundrums seem to blur these calls? Emotional particulars tend to pull us off scriptural point that way. When we clear away the emotional arguments and peripherals, the answers Paul gives us are clear:

1) *When a believer unjustly deserts a believer, the biblical protocol is to sincerely attempt reconciliation.*

2) *When an unbeliever is content to stay with a believer, the believer is to remain in the marriage as a testimony to the unbeliever.*

3) *When an unbeliever chooses to leave a believer, the believer is to let go of the unbeliever. Thereafter, the believer is not under bondage.*

•　　•　　•

CURIOUS ABOUT EXACTLY WHAT "*not under bondage*" means? Unsure what circumstances allow for biblical remarriage? We'll take on those questions in the next chapter.

10

Redeemed Remarriage

"I'd never been married. But when a divorced Christian man began to pursue me, I was counseled to gently check in with him about the circumstances of his divorce. As intentional as he was, it seemed best to find out early on if he were biblically eligible to remarry. Thank God, he was! Our eventual marriage has been a great blessing for both of us."

Is that divorced person-of-interest biblically eligible to remarry? Come to think of it, are you?

These days, it may be rare for believers to ask these important questions. But it's refreshing when they do. As awkward as it may seem to broach this topic in budding relationships, I'm convinced of God's affection for those who not only seek such divine guidance, but also follow it. Especially when it comes to matters of the heart.

Do pre-Christian divorces count?

Grace is an amazing gift. All who are born again are washed in the saving blood of Jesus. All sins of the past are dead and gone, including the sins of past relationships.

Paul wrote this freeing verse to the Corinthians, the same church he instructed about divorce and remarriage:

> *"Therefore, if any man is in Christ, he is a new creature; the old things passed away; behold new things have come [all things have become new]."*
> 2 Corinthians 5:17

The Greek wording of the end of this verse is most consistent with the bracketed ASV translation above, indicating an across-the-board regeneration. This assures us that *all things* are made new upon rebirth. It's a spiritual moment of jubilee when all old debts of sin are canceled.

There are those who believe that divorces prior to salvation still count against the redeemed, but I am not one of them. Each believer must make peace with

God about this call. However, in light of this verse and many others like it, I am persuaded that as long as there are no current marriages, criminal issues, or unmet legal obligations to tend to under the law of the land, the new believer is free from all spiritual encumbrances of past sin.

Clean slate.

Fresh start.

Reborn.

Hallelujah!

We should keep in mind that marriages between unbelievers were not under the biblical covenant. Obtaining a bona fide divorce is a civil matter for the unredeemed. Therefore, any legal divorces that took place prior to regeneration may be considered water under the bridge of grace. They have passed away as part of the comprehensive endowment of spiritual rebirth, never to be held against the believer again.

In getting to know any prospective mate, it's still important to be forthcoming about one's marital history and what led to any pre-Christian divorce. But in light of a person's status as a new creation, such conversations should serve a different purpose.

Sharing our stories should contribute to honest consideration and evaluation of each other's potential compatibility for marriage, no doubt. But there's plenty of biblical room to believe that pre-Christian history needn't impede a first Christian marriage.

Remarriage after a Christian Divorce

For some, vetting a potential mate's remarriageability after a Christian divorce may seem unnecessary—even out of touch with today's practices. They'd rather let bygones be bygones and start with a fresh slate, wiped clean by grace. If the newly redeemed get a clean slate, why can't everyone else?

We should remember, God spoke through the Scriptures to the church. When Moses, Jesus, and Paul said what they said about divorce and remarriage, they specifically addressed those of the household of faith.

Before getting involved with another person after a Christian divorce, take the Bible's counsel to heart. Those who revere God's Word are well advised to consider if a prospective mate is biblically eligible for remarriage. Or even if the circumstances of our own personal histories make marrying again scripturally permissible. As we follow Christ in all these things, we embrace that the Bible's directives are for our protection and good.

Scared to know what the Bible says?

It does take a certain amount of bravery to dig into the Scriptures on remarriage. Particularly if there's a desired relationship at stake, we may be tempted to plug our ears, feign ignorance, and cop a quick plea for grace. That's why I encourage you to remember that God's Word is a lamp to your feet. And the truth the Bible speaks is recorded there with your very best at heart.

So, take courage, Believer.

God is for you.

He is not trying to withhold anything that would be truly good for you. This isn't about legalism. It's about examining what the Bible really has to say, and then honoring your heavenly Father's loving directives. It's about leaning in and trusting Him to know better than we do. That's precisely what this believer did:

> *"When a divorced man began to show an interest in me, I paused to think about it before I let my heart get too involved. I didn't want to assume anything about this great guy, so I asked about the circumstances. As a pastor's daughter and a longtime believer, it was important to me to make sure this man was the innocent spouse in his divorce.*
>
> *As it turned out, he was betrayed by his first wife's adultery, freeing him to remarry. We bonded over our mutual brokenness and I became a bride for the first time. What a wonderful, devoted husband he has been to me. A true gift from God."*

Who knows? When you brave these questions, you might be relieved at what you'll find. Sometimes, God's answers lead us joyfully down the road to matrimony. Sometimes they protectively wave us off contentious heartaches we never would have seen coming. Sometimes, they even save us from the very brink of disaster. They may encourage us to remain satisfied singles.

But whatever you find, trust that your Good Shepherd sees the bigger picture of your life. He loves you enough to guide you away from harm and into safe pastures. There at His feet, you can take the time you need to heal as a newly single person. You can get a sharper perspective on your future by examining your past from an emotional distance.

Circumstances of divorce vary widely. If you fled from a dangerous spouse, the directive to reconcile wouldn't be advisable. But if the divorce came about for other reasons, you may find that the grass isn't quite so green as you thought it would be when you first split with your ex. You may yet reunite.

Remarriage to Your Original Spouse

This is the one type of remarriage the Bible condones for most believers. God set the example in taking His guilty Bride back after divorcing her:

"Return, faithless Israel," declares the LORD; *"I will not look upon you in anger. For I am gracious," declares the* LORD; *"I will not be angry forever."*

Jeremiah 3:12

Whether you were guilty or innocent of breaking the original covenant, as long as there was no intervening marriage, nothing in Scripture prohibits remarriage to one's original spouse. Still, fresh on the heels of divorce, reconciliation might be the last thing on your mind. You may need time to heal, like this friend of mine did:

"As hard as I tried, I couldn't live with the fierceness of his temper. His outbursts cut so deep, shredding me inside. For our daughter's emotional well-being as well as my own, I divorced him. There was never anyone else. We just couldn't live with him anymore. Not the way he was.

Broken and dejected, my ex left for the foreign mission field. When he returned years later, I heard from him. Something sounded different in his voice. He explained that he'd been diagnosed with bipolar depression. Counseling and medication helped him stay on a more consistent emotional keel.

With everything in him, he took responsibility for our failed marriage. Humbly, he asked if I'd

175

> *consider reconciliation. I'll never forget when he said*
> *these words to me: 'I want to take out every sword I*
> *have put into your heart.'*
>
> *Something in me knew this change would be*
> *lasting. Soon, we remarried—this time for good."*

To date, this couple has been successfully remarried far longer than their first time, when I stood up in their wedding. They are a testimony to the miraculous healing grace of God.

Abandoned Spouse of an Unbeliever

Maybe you're a believer who was abandoned by an unbeliever. If so, Paul's directive to the Corinthians applies to you. Here's that verse again:

> *"Yet if the unbelieving one leaves, let him leave; the*
> *brother or the sister is not under bondage in such*
> *cases, but God has called us to peace."*
>
> *1 Corinthians 7:15*

In keeping with the Jewish divorce writ still so familiar in the First Century, the abandoned spouse's status was changed to *unmarried* for the expressed purpose of freeing the betrayed to remarry without being considered guilty of any covenant-breaking sin.

Free Indeed

There's a consensus about almost all of 1 Corinthians 7:15, but there are those who construe it to only allow for divorce, but not for remarriage. In a problematic interpretation, they say that the abandoned should remain single, especially if no adultery has taken place to break the one-flesh bond.

However, when Paul said "*the brother or sister is not under bondage*" in verse 15, his language was abundantly unambiguous. Paul used the Greek word *douloo* to describe what the abandoned believer is not. The word *douloo* speaks of a slave, a person held under bondage, someone who remains the legal property and beholding to another.

Paul used this word *douloo* elsewhere in his letters. In Galatians 4:3–5, he used it to refer to the bondage from which Christ set us free. It speaks of how Jesus redeemed us, conferring upon us a changed legal status as children of God. So, in saying *the believer is not under bondage*, Paul can be correctly understood to mean exactly that.

The believer is free indeed.

Biblically, abandoned believers are no longer bound in any way to their former legal status as married to a deserting, unbelieving ex-spouse. The believer is completely emancipated, legally unbound, rendered free in such cases. Consider just what freedom in Christ looks like for those He has loosed from their bonds:

> *"If therefore the Son shall make you free, you shall be free indeed."*
>
> *John 8:36*

To say the unbound are not eligible to remarry is to say they are still bound by the marriage vows already broken by another. It would be to victimize the innocent spouse all over again. This is not even faithful legalism because it would extend Paul's language beyond its natural meaning.

If the believer is not released from those betrayed marriage bonds, to what else could Paul possibly have been saying the believer is no longer bound? (That's a rhetorical question for which there is no satisfying answer.)

Biblically, there is no binding covenant that could pertain in 1 Corinthians 7:15 other than the marriage covenant itself. Thus, the only possible meaning is that the betrayed innocent spouse is, indeed, set wholly free from those marriage bonds.

In such cases, believers are released from any and all obligations to the marriage vows first broken by an unbeliever's desertion. There is no mandate to seek reconciliation with an unbeliever. There is only Paul's directive to allow the unbeliever to leave.

In setting the abandoned believer free, in addition to the immorality [*porneia*] exception made by Jesus, a new clarification of Mosaic Law was made by Paul. Desertion by an unbeliever became an affirmed New Covenant exception that was deemed as valid biblical grounds for both divorce and remarriage.

This Pauline exception allows the abandoned innocent spouse to move on in the God-given peace to which all believers are called. In citing it, Paul was in full accord with Moses, the Prophets, and Jesus before him.

But even when remarriage is permitted, recovery from marital betrayal shouldn't be rushed. It's wise to really get to know a person before considering remarriage, even after your divorce is final. As old as you may be, it can still take a long while for a person's true colors to show. That's why it's best to give that new relationship the gifts of time and prayer.

Believer Who Deserted a Believer

It's been said that no true believer would ever desert another faithful believer. This is because to do so would be to break with the very faith one claims, to act as an unfaithful person, an unbeliever.

Still, within the household of faith, some find themselves unable to remain wed. The believer who unjustly breaks a marriage covenant by deserting another believer is considered the guilty spouse and will answer to God for the breaking of that covenant. In this case, the remaining spouse is not to blame for the covenant-breaking sin of the deserter.

Concerted efforts toward reconciliation should be made. Counseling should be sought and sincerely considered. Conflict resolution should be attempted in keeping with the pattern Jesus set in Matthew 18:15– 17.

The marriage may seem beyond saving, but miracles of this kind still happen. I've seen multiple marriages beautifully restored, even between believers who've been estranged and remained unmarried for years. Healed relationships have gone on to bear Kingdom fruit.

In keeping with the counsel of Scripture, I encourage all unjust departers to seek reconciliation with their as yet unmarried believing exes.

Meanwhile, believers who unjustly initiated a divorce should guard their hearts from romantic entanglements with others. As lonely as you may feel, do not start dating, even casually.

Stay celibate. Politely refuse attempts of other people who try to set you up with someone new. Instead, I encourage you to make yourself wholly faithful to your marriage vows and available to reconciliation with your believing spouse.

Remarriage after Desertion by a Believer Who Refuses to Reconcile

Theologians differ on when the abandoned innocent is allowed to remarry if the believing deserter refuses to return. Both Mosaic Law and 1 Corinthians 7:11 are conclusive that the deserter should remain single or reconcile, but there's nothing overt about if or how long innocents should allow for reconciliation.

The narrowest view is that innocents must wait to remarry until after the deserter dies, even if the deserter goes on to commit adultery. This legalistic stance negates Mosaic allowances and the exception Jesus made in Matthew 19:9 for immorality.

In a more scripturally inclusive view, some rely on implications from Moses' and Paul's writings. They extrapolate that the desertion-based divorce only obligates the unjust deserter to remain unmarried or reconcile, but sets all innocents free to remarry. Clearly, Paul considered mixed-faith marriages just as binding as marriages between believers. Apparently, he accepted the Jewish divorce writ's allowance for innocents to remarry. That's why many conclude that 1 Corinthians 7:15 implies the innocent may remarry, whether deserted by an unbeliever or a believer.

The most biblically explicit view maintains that abandoned innocents should stay available to reconcile until the deserter breaks the one-flesh bond.

Of course, unless a believing deserter remarries, it may not be clear whether or not the one-flesh bond has been broken. Out of shame, spiritual pride, or even spite, the believing deserter might withhold that pivotal information. This can leave innocents waiting indefinitely. As Paul advised, it's good to remain unmarried, but if unmarried innocents find they can't control their desires, it's better to marry than to fall into sexual sin (1 Corinthians 7:8–9).

Those who wait for confirmation that a believing deserter has broken the one-flesh bond do reap some significant benefits. They avoid rebound relationships and stay single-heartedly receptive to reconciliation. They can recover more fully from the trauma of betrayal. There's also the unassailable assurance of being on the most absolute biblical ground once Jesus' exception explicitly allows remarriage.

Can a believer remarry after initiating an unjust divorce?

Most often, those who ask this question are in the throes of marital discontentment. Though they have complaints about their spouses, none rise to the level of biblically just cause for divorce. In most cases, this believer wants out of a present marriage and looks forward to pursuing another relationship.

If you're asking this question, Jesus loved you enough to give you a straight answer in Matthew 19:9. His answer is compassionate, but it's a firm *no*. Those who are tempted to betray an innocent spouse should recommit themselves to be faithful to their vows.

Believers who have already unjustly broken a Christian marital covenant should reconcile or remain unmarried. If reconciliation isn't possible, they should find godly contentment as celibate singles. Paul affirms the advantages of such a life, wholly devoted to the Lord (1 Corinthians 7:32–35).

This truth may sound harsh.

It might crush you to face it. It may leave you in tears. This is not to minimize the distress you may be feeling. Rather, it is to encourage you to follow the Lord you've given your life to, even when the path He advises isn't the one your flesh wants to follow.

Let Jesus' words encourage you to keep your vows to your innocent spouse. Submit as He firmly closes the door on your temptation.

Believe that this is for your best.

The idea that you'd be happier with someone else is an illusion, a fantasy. Once the thrill of forbidden romance would give way to the reality of day-to-day remarriage, you'd find you've just traded one set of relational challenges for another. In so doing, you would have betrayed your vow to your original spouse and to the Lord. You'd also be guilty of adultery.

As mentioned, even unjust divorce is not the unpardonable sin. You can repent and be forgiven. But there are consequences to such a choice that God exhorts you to accept.

Because of the damage unjust divorce does to the innocent spouse, there is no divinely blessed second chance to keep this lifelong covenant. Those who commit the sin of unjustly divorcing a spouse are not biblically eligible to remarry. See that hard line as the incentive that it is to remain in your marriage.

Instead of identifying with your discontentment, put on the selfless mind of Christ. Identify with the innocent spouse as He does.

Lavish godly affection and respect on your emotionally distant husband. Sacrificially love the wife of your youth as her beauty softens with age. Model faithfulness to your children. Be that larger person that you stood at the altar and promised to be—for better or for worse, for richer or poorer, in sickness and in health—as long as you both shall live.

Widows and Widowers

Though many choose to remain unmarried after the death of a spouse, there are scriptural options. Both widows and widowers are free to remarry any believer who is also biblically eligible for remarriage:

"A wife is bound as long as her husband lives; but if her husband is dead, she is free to be married to whom she wishes, only in the LORD. **40** *But in my opinion she is happier if she remains as she is; and I think that I also have the Spirit of God."*

1 Cor 7: 39–40

Despite Paul's opinion on remarriage prospects in verse 40, he actually recommends remarriage for younger widows in his letter to Timothy:

"Therefore, I want younger widows to get married, bear children, keep house, and give the enemy no occasion for reproach."

1 Timothy 5:14

In context with First Century culture, Paul's advice didn't sound as male-centric as it may today. We should remember that, in Paul's day, women were largely uneducated and rarely worked outside of their own homes or fields.

Unlike career women of today, First Century women depended upon their husbands for those three things Moses required of their husbands (provision, protection, and conjugal cohabitation). Widows quickly found themselves without support, so Paul wrote to Timothy out of compassion for widows, wanting to see to their care.

If we read the surrounding verses, we see that Paul's main point was to advise Timothy about which widows should be put on the list to be supported by the church. Apparently, there were many more widows than Timothy's early church could support. For that reason, Paul wrote instructions geared at serving the truly needy, often older widows first. Others who were younger were encouraged to remarry and be supported by believing men, just as Old Testament widows were.

Paul's advice to Timothy also addressed another problem, the tendency of younger widows to stray into sensuality and idle pursuits. He also recognized that they could still remarry within their childbearing years and make happy homes.

Older Widows and Widowers

Paul's judgment was different for widows over the age of sixty. It seemed necessary to limit the list of which widows the church could afford to support. The line had to be drawn somewhere. Ultimately, Paul advised that widows who qualified should be devoted believers who had served the church and had only been married once. Presumably, those who had remarried had no need to be supported by the church anyway.

There are those who take 1 Timothy 5:9–10 to mean that widows over sixty should not remarry, but Paul made no such limitation. This passage is only meant to specify which widows qualified for the financial support of the church. Granted, as First Century women aged, their marriage prospects dwindled, so the church did what they could to take in those older women who truly needed help. At the same time, all widows remained eligible for remarriage to qualifying believers.

What about the widowers? In light of 1 Timothy 5:8's admonition that those who don't take care of their own are worse than infidels, it's fair to assume that the church also reached out to men in need. And following the death of a spouse, widowers were equally eligible for remarriage within the faith.

What if I'm unjustly remarried?

If you're asking this question, remember that Jesus died for those sins of your past. You are forgiven of every sin you've confessed, even the sin of adultery by unjust remarriage.

While the minority sites Ezra's *putting away* of foreign wives, those were not legal marriages under God. Also, Deuteronomy 24:1–4 forbids returning to a former spouse after a lawful intervening marriage.

Though your union began in sin, it is nonetheless a covenant you've made under God with a new spouse. Upon repentance for that sin, your remarriage is sanctified by Jesus' atoning blood. The price paid for that grace should never be taken lightly.

As Jesus advised in John 8:11, going forward, "*sin no more.*" Do not break faith with your current spouse in an effort to right wrongs that God has forgiven. Remain faithful to the spouse you remarried for life.

Discussion Questions

1) *Is a believer free to divorce and remarry after being deserted by an unbeliever? Justify your answer from Scripture.*

2) *What is the definition of an unbeliever?*

3) *How long should a believer attempt to reconcile after being abandoned by another believer?*

•　　•　　•

STILL WONDERING IF YOU are biblically eligible to divorce or remarry? As you can see, much depends upon the circumstances of a person's divorce. We'll explore scriptural grounds in the next chapter.

11

Holy Grounds

"It wasn't easy to forgive her first affair, but I did. Years later, she secretly drained all our accounts. After I confronted her with proof of another affair, she fell into the habit of hitting me repeatedly whenever I came home. I'd curl my arms over my head to protect myself. When I tried holding her arms just firmly enough to stop her from beating me, she screamed that I was abusing her. Though I never hit her, she poisoned my associates with this lie about me. How can a man defend himself against such utterly false charges? It comforts me that God knows the truth about everything."

There are times when biblical grounds for divorce are devastatingly clear. Like the innocent spouse above, there are multiple scriptural allowances that apply.

Moses, the Prophets, and Jesus concur—this believer had just cause to divorce and remarry.

Then again, there are other times when grounds don't seem so cut and dried. Devoted believers often wrestle with doubt over what might constitute biblical justification for divorce. When they counsel with clergy, responses can be across the board. Inquirers might hear anything from the legalistic opinion that there are no biblical grounds for divorce, to insistence that the only just cause is adultery, to the limited but multiple just-cause stance of this book, to the more liberal "grace covers and allows for all" philosophy.

Perhaps the best way to lead into what are legitimate biblical grounds is to first clear the decks of things that are not. The following statements evidence challenges to living out the marital covenant. In and of themselves, none of these statements represent biblical grounds for divorce or remarriage.

Not Biblical Grounds

- *I don't love him anymore.*
- *We've grown apart.*
- *Someone else "gets" me more.*
- *She let herself go.*
- *My spouse wants to move and I don't.*
- *We argue all the time.*

- *There's no fruit in this marriage.*
- *We can't reconcile our differences.*
- *My spouse became infirmed or disabled.*
- *We don't share the same faith.*
- *There's no romance left.*

These are the cries of a spouse who is biblically advised to stay in and work on the marriage. They are expressions of personal dissatisfaction.

Each statement communicates disappointment in what the speaker is not receiving from the marriage. None address what the speaker is best encouraged to sow into the marriage, exhibiting personal faithfulness to those marriage vows, made before God.

Diagnosis and Treatment

That *Not Grounds* list is by no means exhaustive. Others in this category may come to mind. Cite and discuss scriptural antidotes for each of these *Not Grounds* statements. If someone in your group is struggling with marital discontentment along these lines, offer to come alongside that person. Undergird that believer with encouragement and prayer.

Remember, just because these aren't biblical grounds for divorce doesn't mean that feeling these ways isn't painful. These statements can be symptomatic of significant problems in a marriage. Left untreated, they can be toxic to marital health.

If you're overwhelmed by complaints like these about your spouse, consider Christian marriage counseling. Even good marriages can benefit from a regular tune-up. If going to a licensed counselor isn't feasible for you, try reading some of the many good Christian marriage books out there. Consider pro-active ways that you can be part of your marital solution.

On the other hand, there are times when marriages are violated in far more significant ways. Again, divorce should always be seen as a last resort. But thank God, yes. The Bible does provide a way of escape under specific dire circumstances.

These *Just-Cause Grounds* can be a heavenly lifeline to those who have kept their vows faithfully, yet have found themselves biblically betrayed. No bride or groom ever dreamed to find themselves the victim of anything on the upcoming list of biblically justifiable grounds.

About These Just-Cause Grounds

As noted early on, though the majority of biblical scholarship recognizes most (if not all) of this list as legitimate grounds for a Christian to divorce, there are some minority detractors. Also, keep in mind—while *No Fault* divorce is legal in many places, just-cause Christian divorces must have specific underlying biblical grounds.

Each believer is advised to pore over the Scriptures personally. Allow the Holy Spirit to have the final word in concert with godly counsel. Only you will stand before God to answer for the cause you cite for divorcing a spouse. Do not lean on this or any other humanly authored book. Only rely on the inerrant testimony of the Bible.

None of these grounds should be taken lightly. They shouldn't be charged falsely or frivolously. A genuinely innocent spouse would never hope to have the opportunity to claim such betrayals. True believers would only make these claims if they were honest, and if the situation were beyond any reasonable attempts to reconcile.

The Overall Umbrella of Desertion

All biblical just causes for divorce fall under the broad umbrella of desertion. Whether the one-flesh vow is abandoned via neglect, immorality, treachery, or criminality, at least one of the marital covenants has been forsaken. As sin begets sin, the deserter often breaks the marriage vows on multiple levels.

There are two forms of marital abandonment that can be just cause for the innocent spouse to divorce:

1) Literal desertion
2) Constructive desertion

LITERAL DESERTION is when a spouse actually moves out of the home you've shared with no intent to return within a mutually agreeable time. There are instances when couples agree to trial separations, but deserters abandon the home without such agreements to return. Sometimes literal deserters take their belongings with them. Sometimes they just leave with nothing more than a wallet. But in any case, they abandon the innocent spouse without communicating intent to resume cohabitation.

CONSTRUCTIVE DESERTION can be much more challenging to diagnose. In constructive desertion, the spouse might physically remain at home. But for all practical purposes, he or she has vacated the marriage vows. The constructive deserter either abandons fidelity via sexual immorality, or willfully creates an environment in which the innocent spouse (and any children) cannot financially, legally, or safely remain.

Examples of constructive desertion mirror the same list of covenant-breaking grounds for divorce as literal deserters:

BIBLICALLY JUST CAUSES

1) Neglect / Abandonment

Willful, harmful, and pervasive desertion and/or dereliction of household/marital duties contributing to provision, protection, and conjugal cohabitation; persistent unnecessary absence and/or on-going refusal of marital sexual relations except as limited by disability, or under mutual agreement as a season for prayer (*Exodus 21:10–11, 1 Corinthians 7:3–5*);

2) Indecency / Dishonorable Conduct

Sexual immoralities including fornication, adultery, incest, pedophilia, bestiality, promiscuity, harlotry, unrepentant persistent sexual gratification through pornography, all sexual acts outside the context of biblical marriage; discovery of a disgraceful flaw in conduct, uninhibited substance abuse resulting in marital negligence or harm, failure to submit to reasonable treatment of violent mental illnesses or dangerous disorders (*Deuteronomy 24:1, Matthew 19:9*);

3) Treachery / Violence

Injurious acts against a spouse, children, or others such as murder, disfigurement, terrorism, rape, physical abuse, or pervasive emotional cruelty (*a professional, third-party diagnosis is highly recommended in cases of emotional abuse/cruelty*) (*Malachi 2:10b–11*);

4) Criminal Immorality

Plotting, abetting, and/or commission of violent or nonviolent felonious acts rising to the level of actionable criminal offenses and incarceration; willfully exposing the marital household to harmful prosecution by local police and/or national governing authorities (*includes all unlawful treachery and violence under Malachi 2:10b–11*).

Application

That's quite a list of offenses, isn't it? Let's take a bit of time to digest this list with a short exercise where we'll cite legitimate versus frivolous grounds. If you're doing this exercise with a group, jot your answers down and pass them to your leader to read to the group anonymously. Discuss what others list as legitimate vs. frivolous and why.

Not sure if an offense rises to the level of legitimate just cause for divorce? Note it under *Not Sure*. Use this exercise to gain honest insight from others in your Bible Study. I'll start with the first one.

1) Neglect / Abandonment

Legitimate: *permanently moves out*
Frivolous: *forgets our anniversary*
Not Sure: *needlessly delinquent paying bills*

2) Indecency / Dishonorable Conduct
> Legitimate:
> Frivolous:
> Not sure:

3) Treachery / Violence
> Legitimate:
> Frivolous:
> Not sure:

4) Criminal Immorality
> Legitimate:
> Frivolous:
> Not sure:

The purpose of this exercise is to train our minds to see past any personal challenges and emotional empathies. It helps us discern the difference between covenant-breaking sins and what should be dealt with as petty offenses.

Those frivolous failings of a spouse may be annoying. They may drive you to distraction at times. But as hard as they may be to live with, only the hardhearted would consider them grounds for a Christian to divorce.

To SUM UP THIS SECTION on biblically just causes for divorce, innocent spouses are exhorted to exercise caution and discretion in dealing with covenant breakers, especially those with violent tendencies.

Keep Jesus' words in mind:

> *"Behold, I send you out as sheep in the midst of wolves; therefore be shrewd [wise, discreet] as serpents, and innocent as doves."*
>
> *Matthew 10:16*

As you proceed, keep your heart pure. There is no sin in doing what must be done to secure your household. However, there are ways that we can fall into sin in the process of dealing with the sins of a spouse against us. Consider each item on this list:

1) Refrain from making frivolous or false charges when there is no meaningful breach.

2) Avoid attempts to look for seeming biblical loopholes as a way out of an unhappy marriage.

3) Be reasonable about expectations of a spouse.

4) Except when there is present physical danger, meaningful complaints about persistent sin should be addressed directly with the spouse

first, giving time to address each issue. If the spouse doesn't receive or act on the complaints, follow Matthew 18:15–17's pattern for conflict resolution.

5) Seek Christian counseling when contemplating divorce for any cause.

6) Always forgive, whether recommitting to vows post-betrayal or divorcing.

Whether a grievance is legitimate or frivolous— whether recommitting or divorcing, the truly innocent spouse will maintain a reasonable, forgiving spirit toward an offending spouse.

No matter what course your marriage takes, live as the forgiven believer you are. Interact with uncommon grace. Even with the vilest offender, do everything in that spirit of integrity, humility, wisdom, and mercy that so becomes the redeemed.

•　　•　　•

NEED MORE GUIDANCE for victims of treachery? The next chapter is especially for you. We'll pause from studying the Bible to consider some specific counsel.

12

Marital Treachery

She was warned after her husband seriously injured her the first time. He said it was an accident, but that's how he'd explained his first wife's death. By then, there had been far too many lies to trust another word he said. Over more than a year, she began to pave a way of escape. Covertly, she opened her own bank and email accounts. She got a secret phone he couldn't monitor. But when he surprised her with a romantic getaway, how could she refuse to go?

Tragically, this believing wife didn't live to tell the story of that harrowing weekend. Again, her spouse insisted that her death was a terrible accident. He said he was a loving Christian husband, that he would never do such a thing. Evidence mounted against him. Forged life insurance policies emerged. In a case that made headlines across the globe, this man has since been convicted of his wife's murder.

Thousands of years ago, Moses found himself dealing with much the same thing amongst God's people. Some wayward husbands simply *put away* neglected wives to avoid paying back their dowries. As if that weren't bad enough, others devised ways to murder their wives and make it look like an accident. That's why Moses was inspired to permit divorce and to require certain standards—to prevent the greater evil of marital treachery that could befall the innocent spouse.

This is the same reason God railed at Israel's priests that He hated *putting away* and those men who covered themselves with violence (Malachi 2:14–16). And when innocent spouses divorce such treacherous spouses, they're standing on solid holy grounds, in the way of escape offered by their Maker.

Previously in this study, we've touched on the sin of marital treachery as just cause for divorce. Because this particular mode of unfaithfulness can be so damaging, even lethal to the innocent spouse, we'll spend a bit more time examining various forms of it, including the violence that takes place through both physical and emotional abuse by a spouse. We'll also touch on steps innocent spouses in this position may contemplate.

First, let's consider the plight of those who find themselves in physical danger.

Marital Violence

When a married person perishes under suspicious circumstances, there's a good reason detectives always investigate the surviving spouse first. All too often, even those who claim some measure of faith are proven guilty of slaying the spouse they've vowed to protect.

It's chillingly common.

Still, innocent spouses in very real peril are discouraged by some churches from leaving violent spouses. Too often, religious people tell the innocent spouse that it would be a sin to divorce for any cause other than adultery. They misquote the original language of Malachi by advising that God hates [divorce]. They say to stay and pray, even after severe beatings, blatant threats, or attempts on an innocent spouse's life.

The problem with dealing with a physically abusive spouse or a psychopath is that one never knows when treachery will strike next. Between incidents, things seem to return to normal. The honeymoon period after a life-threatening event can go on for weeks or months, before the next eruption.

Apologies are made.

Promises are profuse.

Life goes on quietly for a season.

As the wolf slyly dons sheep's clothing once more, the innocent spouse is lulled into a false sense of security. The lines blur, to the point where innocents wonder if they have real grounds anymore.

Maybe my wife has changed, he might hope. *Maybe those prayers for my husband have been answered*, she supposes. Until that ticking time bomb of rage explodes once again. Sometimes with lethal impact.

This is deadly serious.

As someone who has attended one too many funerals of Christian victims of marital violence, I plead with all who are innocent of such treachery to hear me. If your wife has attempted to kill you once, she has been unfaithful to her marital covenant with you. The moment your husband physically injures you in anger, he has constructively deserted you, giving you biblical cause to divorce.

What if it's just a threat?

This depends on the nature of the threat. There's that awful hyperbolic expression—"*I'm going to kill you!*"— usually said in jest and not meant to be taken literally. But if a raging spouse credibly threatens to kill you or raises a lethal weapon against you, you have just cause to flee for your life (at your first safe opportunity).

What if it doesn't go that far? Say your spouse raises a hand to you, but finds the strength to back down. Because your spouse demonstrated sufficient self-control to resist the urge to strike you, there may be hope.

After the rage has passed, calmly put your spouse on notice that you have a zero tolerance policy when it comes to physical assault. Clearly voice your intent to leave after even one such violent attack. At the same time, assure your spouse of your love. Voice your desire to stay married as long as you remain safe. Suggest that you go to marriage counseling together. If your spouse agrees, arrange for professional help as soon as possible.

What should violence victims do?

If your spouse intentionally injures you, there is no need to offer the abuser another chance or warning, even if the abuser claims to be a believer. Why? Because your spouse has already broken the Bible's mandate to protect you, and thereby been unfaithful.

Most likely, unless an abuser sincerely submits to on-going professional counseling and meaningful spiritual intervention, the attacks will be repeated and could escalate in frequency and force. If you stay after even one injurious physical assault, you will probably be assaulted again, even more severely.

Take this seriously.

You could be at risk for your life.

For your personal safely—wisdom and discretion are advised. Your life is of far more value than anything you stand to lose by leaving a spouse who mercilessly beats you. He may say it's your fault. She may claim you drove her to it. Do not listen to these classic lies told by abusers. Instead consider taking these basic steps:

1) Get through the violent attack.

In the midst of the assault, call out to God for help within your spirit. Even if you feel entitled, do not provoke more attacks by verbal or physical retaliation. Refrain from announcing any plan to leave (Proverbs 15:1). Go for a walk if you can. If you must return, wait at least 30 minutes for tempers to cool first.

2) Stop covering for your abuser.

Quietly document all injuries. Seek medical attention if necessary. If you haven't already, break the silence with your pastor, your family, a trusted friend of your own gender, and a Christian counselor. If you can't afford paid counseling, call a domestic abuse help line. Be discreet in all communications about your ex.

3) Plan your escape.

Wait just long enough for an opportune time when your abuser is gone to make your escape. (If you have children, consult an authority about legalities to observe in securing your children.) Take only essentials. Your heavenly Father knows exactly what you need. Trust Him to provide for you while you wait for more permanent living arrangements to be settled.

4) Take refuge.

Go to a safe house or a designated shelter for refuge. Even if you feel you have a right to kick the abuser out of your home, take separate shelter until the unsafe situation is stabilized. Do not let the abuser know where you are. Turn off any tracking devices on your phone, computer, or car.

5) Call 9-1-1.

As soon as you're in a secure place, contact the police. Officially report all incidents of domestic violence. Give the police copies of any hospital reports and/or injury photos. Carefully consider if it is advisable to get a restraining order. Though restraining orders are meant to protect you, they are frequently violated and may exacerbate an already volatile situation. On the other hand, they may serve as a deterrent to contact, depending upon your circumstances.

6) Seek professional assistance.

Meet with professionals who can help you sort out what's best to do given your specific situation. If you can't afford a lawyer, apply for charitable legal aid. Allow a Christian counselor to assist you in your emotional recovery from the trauma you have suffered.

7) Be discreet.

For your own safety, refrain from using any traceable communications or credit cards known to your abuser. Resist any urge to interact via social media. Change any of your account passwords your abuser may know. Keep your cell phone off or change your number. Communiqués from your abuser will likely attempt to lure you back with effusive apologies. Save any messages in which your abuser admits to injuring you (as evidence). But do not respond personally—no matter how your abuser may push your buttons or goad you to reply.

8) Insist on an intermediary presence.

Do not go anywhere alone to meet with a violent spouse. This is not about being paranoid. It is about maintaining an appropriate guard with a violent person. Be highly cautious about using your loved ones as a shield. The violent may turn on your family or friends for protecting you.

If you need to pick up personal belongings from your home, hire a professional security guard to accompany you. Choose a time when your abuser is most likely to be at work or away.

Maybe your abuser is a first-time offender and seems unlikely to harm anyone during this process. Even so, it is still safest to meet with clergy, a professional counselor, or a lawyer. Always make sure you have a protective, objective intermediary present as you resolve practical and legal aspects of your lives going forward.

Emotional Abuse

It's been said that angry words can cut deeper than any knife. Scars of emotional cruelty can be just as savage as any beating.

Yet questions persist.

Your wife may have a hot temper. Your husband may blurt hurtful things from time to time. But what's the difference between even heated arguments and emotional abuse? When do emotional cruelties rise to the level of marital treachery?

Sometimes, it sounds something like this:

"You're such an idiot! No wonder you can't get a better job," she screamed after my co-worker got

> *promoted. Since she controlled our finances, she'd buy whatever she wanted, then throw a fit if I spent a penny without her permission. In public or private, she'd loudly berate me over the smallest of infractions, exploding for hours over practically nothing. She'd harp on me in front of family and friends. My off-work hours and even my phone calls and emails were closely monitored. My wife was the puppet master, critically yanking my strings at every turn. 'You'd never make it without me,' she'd accuse. 'You're worthless. A failure. You're going insane.' Though I tried to shut those constant tirades out, eventually I began to believe them."*

That's just a tiny glimpse into the kind of pervasive emotional abuse some innocent spouses suffer. It's more than an occasional outburst of anger or hurtful words here and there. It's a lifestyle of systematic psychological assault. It's the sort of emotional cruelty that keeps its victims isolated, walking on eggshells round-the-clock, terrified of setting off another rage. Abusers may even gaslight, calling their sane victims' mental health into question.

Emotional abuse is a comprehensive form of mental slavery, foisted on a spouse as a captive audience. It's the enemy using a human being to do his dirty work as the accuser of the brethren. It cuts its victims to the core, often leaving permanent scars.

What characterizes emotional abuse?

The classic emotional abuser consistently berates, dominates, controls, de-socializes, isolates, verbally bullies, gaslights, intimidates, mocks, insults, derides, and criticizes. Over time, these cruelties can undermine the hearer's confidence and erode self-esteem at harmful psychological levels.

Unchecked, damage done can be lasting. When persistent, emotional abuse can rise to the level of constructive desertion, injuring and/or seriously threatening the emotional health and safety of a spouse and any children.

> *"I know a woman who remained in such an emotionally abusive marriage. She recognized the systematic way her husband raged at, intimidated, isolated, berated, manipulated, and controlled her. Still, she respected the vows she'd made to God to stay with that man for better or for worse.*
>
> *When she married him, she was a vibrantly independent, confident world traveler and musician. Over the decades, the abuse she suffered profoundly eroded her psyche. She never lost her faith. But by the time her abuser pre-deceased her, she was a mere shadow of her former self—anxiety ridden, paranoid, and agoraphobic. The resonant instrument that had graced stages across the globe*

was silenced. Her loved ones hoped she would recover enough to enjoy her twilight years. But sadly, she never did. The psychological damage was too deep."

Is a believer biblically obligated to remain in such a damaging relationship? Despite the psychological wounds an emotionally abusive spouse can inflict, for many, the call seems unclear when it comes to emotional forms of treachery. It can be one of those gray areas we wrestle over.

When do things cross the line from petty argumentativeness to full-on emotional abuse? If you're asking this question, I encourage you to consult a Christian counselor to objectively assess your situation and any impact this is having on your emotional and mental health.

Physical blows can be readily observed and documented. Emotional scars compound inwardly, yet they can be every bit as real. The danger is increased the longer exposure to abuse persists. Unchecked, abusers get worse over time, leaving innocents less and less equipped to cope with or escape their abusers as they age.

Pervasive emotional abusers are constructive deserters. They create a highly toxic atmosphere that is hazardous to the psychological health and welfare of the innocent spouse and any children. Third-party diagnosis and counsel is essential in such cases.

What if it seems more spotty than pervasive?

A spouse's behavior may border on some aspects of emotional abuse now and then without living that way fulltime. Believers should be discerning and fair in their assessments of each other.

Hot-tempered spouses with low impulse control are particularly inclined to shout caustic barbs on occasion. That doesn't excuse the offense. But they shouldn't automatically be labeled comprehensive emotional abusers, even if those infrequent incidents are hurtful.

Know that a marriage can survive and become healthier, despite intermittent angry outbursts. This is especially the case when both spouses are able to forgive and work at ways to modify hurtful behavior going forward. Objective mediation can help.

Innocent spouses should remain prayerful and Christ-like in marriages with these periodically harsh episodes. Consider this encouragement from the Apostle Peter:

> *"And who is there to harm you if you prove zealous for what is good?* **14** *But even if you should suffer for the sake of righteousness, you are blessed. And do not fear their intimidation, and do not be troubled,* **15** *but sanctify Christ as Lord in your*

> *hearts...yet with gentleness and reverence;* **16** *and keep a good conscience so that in the thing in which you are slandered, those who revile your good behavior in Christ may be put to shame."*
>
> *1 Peter 3:13–16*

Particularly if your believing spouse is sorry enough to address the problem, that godly sorrow is a sign that God is still at work. As Peter noted, when you maintain a gentle and quiet spirit in the midst of harsh treatment, your Christ-like behavior partners with the Holy Spirit to do the good work of bringing conviction to your accuser. The resulting shame can lead to godly repentance and reconciliation.

Is it easy to remain calm in the midst of such storms? Not at first. Denying that reflex to fight back, to defend, and sling barbs of our own is what comes most naturally. But that is the way of the flesh, not the Spirit. Peter's counsel to wives is just as applicable to husbands:

> *"But let it be the hidden person of the heart, with the imperishable quality of a gentle and quiet spirit, which is precious in the sight of God."*
>
> *1 Peter 3:4*

Responding with that grace that is so pleasing to God takes practice. It's like working a muscle. Each time you resist the flesh and give way to the Spirit, the muscle tone of your spirit gets stronger. In time, it actually gets easier to ride through such storms with Jesus than to fret over them like the disciples did. You'll find that the storms pass more quickly if you pray your way through them.

No matter what, do not surrender the peace God has given you in the Spirit. Even as you endure harsh treatment, acknowledge that your Savior is with you, holding His loving hands around your heart. Patiently wait till those lightning bolts cease and that dark cloud passes. Peacefully reassess the relationship.

Good News about Emotional Abuse

Gratefully, emotional abuse doesn't always reach the point of no return. Relational rehabilitation really is possible, particularly if the perpetrator is willing to submit to transparent mediation with a Christian counselor. Objective professionals can help identify the extent and root causes of conflict. Therapy can also help nip unhealthy tendencies in the bud.

Destructive patterns aren't changed overnight. But they can be rehabilitated through consistent counsel, devoted effort and, most of all, prayer. I've seen dysfunctional relationships like this turned completely around.

Miracles can and do still happen when both spouses are willing to identify this problem and love each other enough to work at it. Relationships can be healed and Christian marriages restored through God's redemptive power.

Criminal Desertion

Whenever a spouse chooses to abet or commit a serious crime, another form of constructive desertion occurs. (Countries where the law forces unbiblical acts are an exception, like when Daniel broke the law of the land by continuing to worship only God. That's why each "criminal" act must be evaluated in light of God's higher Law.)

In knowingly committing felonious acts, the criminal spouse fails to provide a safe, legal home-life for the innocent. That's constructive desertion. The criminal exposes the innocent to prosecution and incarceration that may remove the perpetrator from the dwelling against his or her will, effectively causing literal desertion.

It may be that a believer's spouse breaks the law in petty ways not rising to grounds for divorce. This is not to excuse lesser infractions such as violating the speed limit or jaywalking. Believers are biblically advised to be exemplary, law-abiding citizens. But when serious crimes are committed by one spouse, it creates an equally serious problem for both.

Even petty crimes can be a relational red flag. They signal eroding character. Once a person lets lesser forms of integrity slide, things can snowball from there. Remember that man convicted of murdering his wife at the beginning of this chapter? There were warnings. Lies became all too frequent. He was arrested on a minor theft charge. Still, this man claimed to be a believer. His immoral behavior escalated unchecked, leading up to his conviction for murdering his innocent spouse.

Other crimes may not go so far, but still threaten the security of a household in meaningful ways. What if a spouse does business under the table to evade taxes (punishable by prison time)? How should a believer respond to a spouse's embezzlement, Ponzi scheme, sex trafficking, bomb building, or illegal drug-running activities?

Seriously.

Should a believer stay silent after discovering a spouse's homicidal plot?

There's a reasonable line between keeping a spouse's confidences and abetting their crimes. When a spouse plots and/or commits a serious crime, that line gets crossed. Both the law of the land and the marital covenant are broken by the criminal. Even if they remain at home, it's constructive desertion.

Believers in such marriages should exercise extreme caution and discretion. Confide only in trustworthy helpers who need to know. For your own safety and the well-being of any children, such crimes should be reported to the proper authorities. While not guilty of the primary crime, a silent innocent can become subject to charges of abetting illegal activities, impeding an investigation, harboring a fugitive, or being an accessory after the fact.

One spouse cannot be compelled to testify against the other spouse. But there are instances where it is wise to do so voluntarily. Enlist the help of authorities and seek confidential assistance from your church family.

You may still be struggling with remorse over marrying this person. You may be bludgeoning yourself over getting into this position by wedding an unbeliever. But yes, God will help you. That's what's so amazing about grace.

Jesus paid the debt for any failure you've confessed. Think of your ever-loving heavenly Father reaching out to you, as He spoke through the prophet Isaiah:

"And I said to you, 'You are My servant, I have chosen you and not rejected you. **10** *Do not fear, for I am with you. Do not anxiously look about you, for I am your God. I will strengthen you, surely I*

will help you. Surely, I will uphold you with My righteous right hand.' **11** *Behold, all those who are angered at you will be shamed and dishonored. Those who contend with you will be as nothing, and will perish.* **12** *You will seek those who quarrel with you, but will not find them. Those who war with you will be as nothing, and nonexistent.* **13** *For I am the* LORD *your God, who upholds your right hand, who says to you, 'Do not fear, I will help you.'"*

Isaiah 41:9–13

What a glorious refuge this passage is in times of trouble! Do not fear. Take God's outstretched hand. Let Him lead you through the Red Sea of your treacherous marital circumstance. In due time, He will deal with those who have wronged you. Your job is to walk forward, eyes fixed on your Savior as He leads you out of Egypt and into the safety of renewed life.

•   •   •

WOULD YOU LIKE MORE INSIGHT into why your heavenly Father's heart beats with such compassion for every innocent spouse? Join me in acknowledging His amazing grace in the following afterword.

Afterword

Empathy and Grace

"My soul, my soul! I am in anguish! Oh my heart! My heart is pounding in Me; I cannot be silent."

Jeremiah 4:19

In the midst of our own relational traumas, we don't often stop to consider the travail of God's heart over the unfaithfulness that He has endured. He's suffered so much more than we have at the hands of those He has wedded unto Himself.

Reading through Jeremiah gives us a glimpse at the searing emotions our heavenly Father weathers. He endures this repeatedly, each time we betray Him.

Why does God hate *putting away*, that evil perpetrated against sincere believers? Because He knows—all too well—what it's like to be the completely innocent spouse. He's been the victim of neglect, disgraceful actions, treachery, immorality, adultery, idolatry, and desertion.

Repeatedly.

In ways more devastating than we can imagine, our loving God has suffered. Dearly. He must watch our unfaithfulness as it unfolds before His eyes. What's more, think how He must dread the anguish divorce brings upon His innocent children. With hearing more acute than any earthly parent, He listens as our desperate cries reach His understanding ears.

Why does God empathize so deeply with the plight of the innocent spouse? A walk in Jesus' well-worn sandals may help us understand. It may give us a visceral sense of how deeply our heavenly Husband relates to marital suffering.

Meditate on this: at Calvary, Jesus was the ultimate innocent spouse. Jesus was the victim of every just biblical cause for divorce listed here:

Neglect (Luke 22:39–46)

- Ignored: *Jesus was disregarded by those who slept instead of praying as He faced the horror of the cross.*

Dishonorable Conduct (Hebrews 12:2)

- Immorality: *As a spotless sacrificial Lamb, Jesus willingly bore the disgraceful sins, dishonorable character flaws, and shameful indecencies of all human vow-breakers.*

Unfaithfulness (Matthew 26:48–49, 27:1)

- <u>Harlotry</u>: *With a kiss, an intimate friend betrayed Jesus for money.*

- <u>Idolatry</u>: *Jesus suffered under the plots of religious people who were more devoted to their positions and traditions than to the God they'd pledged to serve.*

Treachery (Mark 15:16–20)

- <u>Physical abuse</u>: *Jesus was savagely scourged and mercilessly beaten for our sin.*

- <u>Emotional abuse</u>: *Jesus was unfairly and cruelly criticized, lied about, insulted, berated, desocialized, mocked, and isolated.*

- <u>Criminal acts</u>: *Jesus was violently crucified under false charges leveled by religious wolves in sheep's clothing.*

Desertion (Mark 14:50, Matthew 26:69–75)

- <u>Literal Desertion</u>: *The men closest to Jesus fled, abandoning Him.*

- <u>Constructive Desertion</u>: *Peter repeatedly denied even knowing Jesus.*

•   •   •

YES, GOD HATES THE RAVAGES of marital betrayal and the treacheries leading to divorce. This outpouring of divine empathy is all because of His overwhelming compassion for the betrayed.

Having divorced Israel, our God is the only truly sinless divorcé. And God takes up the cause of the innocent spouse with relevant first-hand experience. He's done so throughout the entire counsel of Scripture—from Genesis, to Moses and the Prophets, through His only Son, Jesus, and throughout the New Testament.

It all comes together as one harmonious love letter to His beloved church.

The Bible's Big Picture about Divorce

Over the course of this study, we've covered a lot of biblical ground in detail. As we close, we can sum up what we've learned with a few short statements:

1) To permit "any cause" divorce is to side with rabbi Hillel and fall into the error of lawlessness, also known as license.

2) To permit divorce only in cases of adultery is to side with rabbi Shammai and fall into the error of legalism.

3) To follow Jesus is to uphold the Spirit of the Law as revealed in the entire prophetic counsel of Scripture in its original language and context, permitting divorce for specific just causes for the sake of the innocent spouse.

4) To reconcile whenever possible is to be like our Father and to flow in the fruit of the Holy Spirit. And to always forgive with the grace we've been given is to live in the light of the new commandment of Jesus: the Law of Love:

"A new commandment I give to you, that you love one another, even as I have loved you, that you also love one another. **35** *By this all men will know that you are My disciples, if you have love for one another."*

John 13:34–35

Indeed, it is God's saving grace that the Bible allows divorce and remarriage when another has broken the one-flesh covenant. This provision is not to grant license to betrayers, but altogether for the sake of the betrayed, when fallen men and women violate marital vows.

God's perfect will and ideals remain unchanged. Nothing would make our heavenly Father happier than if believing husbands and wives would cleave in love, faithfully keeping their covenants to love, honor, and keep each other in each of these exemplary ways:

> *"Love is patient, love is kind, and is not jealous; love does not brag and is not arrogant, does not act unbecomingly; it does not seek its own, is not provoked, does not take into account a wrong suffered, does not rejoice in unrighteousness, but rejoices with the truth; bears all things, believes all things, hopes all things, endures all things. Love never fails."*
>
> *1 Corinthians 13:4–8a*

The truly innocent spouse will look at his or her mate through the lens of Christ's forgiveness and grace, deferring in humble reverence.

> *"...and all of you, clothe yourselves with humility toward one another, for God is opposed to the proud but gives grace to the humble."*
>
> *1 Peter 5:5b*

That honorable marriage so pleasing in God's sight will thrive in mutual submission. For better or for worse, husbands and wives will sacrificially give their lives for each other, just as Christ gave Himself for the church. These holy covenants will go on, either till death parts us, or when His faithful church rises in grace as His eternal spotless Bride.

> *"And be subject to one another in the fear of Christ. Wives, be subject to your own husbands, as to the Lord...* **25** *Husbands love your wives, just as Christ also loved the church and gave Himself up for her...* **27** *that He might present to Himself the church in all her glory, having no spot or wrinkle or any such thing; but that she should be holy and blameless...* **31** *For this cause a man shall leave his father and mother, and shall cleave to his wife; and the two shall become one flesh.* **32** *This mystery is great, but I am speaking with reference to Christ and the church."*
>
> *Ephesians 5:21–22, 25, 27, 31–32*

INSPIRATIONAL BOOKS & MEDIA

About the Author

CHRISTIAN KEEL is a long-married believer as well as an avid student and teacher of the Bible. Keel enjoys playing with dogs during leisurely walks, working from home, getting together with friends, travels across the globe, and following Jesus' calling to be a fisher of men—all in the company of a beloved spouse.

STRAIGHT TALK BIBLE STUDIES provide balanced Christian counsel to those seeking to apply insights from Scripture to contemporary life.

Also by Christian Keel

STRAIGHT TALK BIBLE STUDY • BOOK TWO

IN SHEEP'S CLOTHING

VETTING CHRISTIAN RELATIONSHIPS

Available in Print and Kindle Editions
For Individual or Group Studies

• • •

Thank you, Dear Reader

Please know how much I appreciate the time you've taken to study this topic from God's Word with me.

If you have a moment, would you be so kind as to post a quick review on Amazon? Your feedback is so helpful to me and other readers.

By God's grace,
Christian Keel

• • •

Made in the USA
Coppell, TX
02 July 2023